John Andrews was born
Catholic army family. He
New River in London. A
including *Classic Angling*
contributor to BBC R
currently working on his second book.

— — —

FOR ALL THOSE LEFT BEHIND

Longlisted for the
William Hill Sports Book of the Year 2002

Shortlisted for the
Ladbrokes/NSC Best New Writer of the Year 2003

Shortlisted for the
Angling Writers Association Book of the Year 2003

'Andrews writes fluently, with colour, vision and an eye
for detail. He writes from the heart, perhaps for all
those who have lost loved ones.' Keith Elliott, *Classic
Angling*

'This beautifully written book celebrates the bond of
father and son. It grieves for the separation that
mortality brings to us all and reveals how through
fishing, those we have lost can live on side by side on
the bank.' Helen Stiles, *The Field*

'Read this.' *Independent on Sunday*

'A reassuringly different angling book. Its international
flavour encapsulates all that is wonderful about fishing.
An excellent and intriguing read.' John Wilson, *Sunday
Express*

'As an examination of why we go fishing, this book
stands up as well as any other.' Paul Dennis, *Anglers Mail*

'If you are expecting a book purely about fishing then you would be disappointed, but sure enough there are enough descriptions of angling days and ways that we as anglers can all relate to. However, this book is much more than that.' Steve Ormrod, *Pikelines* (the Pike Anglers Club of Great Britain quarterly)

'I believe this is a major new work in angling literature. First editions will be sought after in years to come. It is a 'must read' for all anglers.' Chris Plumb, *anglersnet.com*

'Looking at *For All Those Left Behind* with its moody illustration of a solitary angler, you'd never guess it was the work of a man that used to help run Creation Records, discoverers of Oasis. John Andrews wrote this highly affecting fishing memoir, set on Skye and elsewhere, as a way of belatedly dealing with the death of his father.' *Caledonia*

'I can recommend this well-presented book, confident that it will provide a good read for many anglers this Christmas and beyond.' John Nunn, the *Norfolk Anglers Conservation Association Journal*

Acknowledgements

My wife Deborah, Graham Haworth, Henry Sutton, the Montigny Resistance and all those who cajoled and encouraged me.

David Smith at Annette Green Authors Agency and all at Mainstream Publishing.

Jon Ward Allen at Waterlog for help in tracing Edward Ensom.

John Richardson for the dust jacket illustration.

A sincere thank you to all members of my family for giving me the grace to tell this story.

For All Those Left Behind

John Andrews

MAINSTREAM
PUBLISHING

EDINBURGH AND LONDON

First published in Great Britain 2002 by
MAINSTREAM PUBLISHING (EDINBURGH) LTD
7 Albany Street
Edinburgh EH1 3UG

ISBN 1 84018 800 6

This edition, 2003

A catalogue record for this book is available from the British Library

Typeset in Chancery and Van Djick

Printed in Great Britain by
Creative Print and Design Wales

In memory of
my father

Chapter One

It was the summer of 1977. I was eleven years old. I was on a family holiday of sorts. My brother and sisters weren't with us, it was just me and my mum and dad. We'd travelled to the Isle of Skye via Derby, where we'd stayed in the house of my football-mad great aunt; and Stirling, where my dad had once been to school as a child. I remember the buses outside my aunt's house, blue double-deckers; her horn-rimmed spectacles; and also the price of a bath in Stirling – fifty pence for the plug.

It was the summer following the great discovery that my father and I both loved going fishing together. I'm sure a bit of him planned the holiday so that we could take full advantage of the coast, then pretty much unspoilt. We stayed in a cottage in the village of Broadford on the east of the island. No sooner had we arrived than my father and I walked down to the jetty. It stuck out into the bay like a broken stone tooth. The water was flat-calm, thick like oil, sleepily low tidal. The bay was shrouded in a summer haze and the air was full of midges. The smell of salt and seaweed was rank and filled our throats. Off the end of the jetty there was some deeper water and in it you could just make out the shapes of fish as their shadows crept in and out of the rocks and pools beneath us. We stayed, watching, for as long as the midges would allow, before returning to the cottage for the staple diet of my childhood – cheese on toast, washed down with a gallon of tea.

The next morning I remember being woken by my father, urging me to get up, as he left the room. Still half asleep I didn't see him but I could hear his voice as he descended the stairs. On my bedside table sat a steaming mug of tea, his morning calling card. He made tea for all of us, religiously, even if we didn't want it; indeed my sister Gill never drank it in the mornings I seem to recall, but Dad made it for her anyway. For sixteen years. One day she might change her mind. He was like that, an unfailing optimist. Once I had woken up I had that confusion that you feel on waking in a strange and unfamiliar place, but as my eyes flicked round the room I realised where I was. The smell of bacon and cigarettes rose up the stairs and the absence of Old Spice mixed in with it told me that this was most definitely a holiday. That and the view from the window. The haze of the previous night had been stripped away by brilliant morning sunshine and the stale saltiness of the air was replaced by a fresh offshore breeze that seemed to go on forever, blowing across the bay and out to the endless horizon.

Sightseeing as such was never on the agenda for me as a child on holiday. A state of normal life would be imposed, one without the routine of work or school to interrupt it, and Mum continued to cook and clean for England. Dad and I hung out, all that was different was that we ate off strange plates and sat in front of open fires. There were outings of a sort. Invariably it would rain and we'd sit in the car, with the windows misting up from the flask as the fruitcake was passed round. I think that our walks and excursions were just an excuse for that, the classic '70s car-bound picnic, always finished off with the words, 'Well, I suppose we ought to be getting back.' Life was on hold for my parents' generation; they had spent five years of broken family mealtimes in the war and they seemed determined to make up for it, to suspend time in that perfect moment of reverie. I had no problem with that, I loved my food as much as the next child, but this was thirty years on and I needed some convincing that bananas were still on the black market and that every rabbit was worth shooting.

Hanging out with my father often meant watching him, whilst he did another one of his endless lists of chores and jobs. It was as if he was in a permanent state of alert, constantly checking that the hatches were battened down and we were ready for the incoming invasion. It had never happened of course, but Dad was always quick to point out that the dressing-gown he wore had come back with his father from Dunkirk. Perhaps that's why Dad was always up at 6 a.m., dressed in that same garment, swigging tea and listening to Hindi hits on the World Service. A sort of colonial suburban home guard.

Today, there was no dressing-gown, and the World Service was muffled by the presence of the Cuillin mountains that rose up behind our cottage. Dad was fully dressed when I got down to breakfast, wearing a Deanesque reversible towelling jacket, old trousers and his wellington boots. He chivvied me along, despairing at my inability to get moving and said he'd wait for me outside. We were going to look for bait.

The tide really had gone out this time and the floor of the sea opened up in front of us. The jetty was stranded but for the last few yards which clung to the retreating sea. A narrow beach stretched the length of the back of the bay. One or two houses stood beyond the road that ran above the beach and an old stone church, spartan and foreboding, dominated proceedings. On the opposite side of the bay, rocks gave way to a rolling hillside. We explored the beach and picked in and out of the rock pools, chipping mussels off the rocks with our knives and soon filling the bucket. The tide had begun to turn and we stood back on the shore and watched it roll in stealthily, covering all the pools and nooks we had been walking over minutes earlier. The day set a pattern for us both. A walk to the beach when the tide was low to find our bait, and then a wait of a few hours until the water was deep enough for us to fish off the jetty wall.

We tackled up back at the house. I'd seen it all before, but this was the first time I would be fishing with any knowledge or confidence. My rod was an eight-foot, luminous green, fibreglass spinning rod, the type that got sold in any seaside shop around our coast. I don't know when my father had bought this particular model but it had followed us on holidays for at least a couple of years. I have no memory of fishing at sea before this time, which is strange because there are photos which suggest otherwise. Perhaps it was because this fortnight seemed to be dedicated to fishing and little else in between. My father's rod was an old split-cane boat fishing rod with a marvellous machine-carved, black wooden handle.

Its old rod rings were attached with a black whipping and the whole thing had the appearance of an elaborate cosh. My reel was a small, fixed-spool reel in electric-fin blue, almost silver. The spool was very shallow so it could only hold about fifty metres of line, but I was assured that this would be enough. Dad's was a blue fixed-spool number which was packed with salty white monofilament line. Corrosion had started around the edges of the reel casing and on the bail arm. I can still picture my father sitting under a lamp in the cottage, cans of pale ale and three-in-one oil weighing down the map of the island on the table as he tinkered with the workings of the mechanism. And then there were the floats. These were stored in the boxes which had supplied the reels and reeked of oil and salt. Mostly made from balsa and cork, with bright-orange tops, a white stripe across the middle and bottle-green or blue bottoms, they had a magical presence all of their own.

It was the first day of proper fishing. The tide had risen fully and it was now afternoon. The clear blue sky of the morning had given way to a blanket of low, grey cloud, which spilled down from the boiling peaks of the Cuillins. You could no longer make out the peaks, just a shroud of steam around the cloud base, split by the promise of light above. In the gloom, the colours of the landscape intensified. The hills were verdant and all over them burnt red bracken ran in huge swathes. Dad and I stood side by side on the wall of the jetty. I wondered what had happened to the crystal-clear water of the previous day. An oily green surface lay flattened by the lowering barometric pressure, swelling gently against the stones with regular slaps. We opened the mussels up with a

11

knife. Their hearts were brilliantly orange. A simple paternoster would carry them down into the water.

The first bite. I hadn't had to wait long. The top of the float tweaked and then pulled under the surface and out of view. I jabbed the top of the rod up hard and it sprang back round with several short stabs. Playing the fish was not an option. I was too excited and simply winched the victim up the wall and onto our feet. A coalfish. About a pound, a pound and a half, with tiny silvery-blue scales, large brown eyes and a white line running along its flank to its tail. My father hit it across his knuckles and its fins shook as it expired. I couldn't bait up and get back in the water quickly enough. Moments later the process repeated itself and up came another obliging coalfish. Soon, we had four or five in the bag. And then the bites stopped as suddenly as they had started. The orange top of my float and the yellow one of my father's sat, bobbing up and down only yards from one another. Our shadows peered down on top of them, blurred by the movement of the water. We stood watching, becoming mesmerised with each second as our smiles and laughter distorted in the growing waves.

We fished like this for days, the time weaving itself into a blur of contentment. I could have carried on living like this forever. There was a tranquillity and reverence to the time we spent there together. On the Sunday my father announced that perhaps I should go out by myself as he had things he needed to sort out. Things he needed to sort out? How could you have things to sort out on a holiday? But I knew him too well to dispute it. There was probably a loose drainpipe on the cottage or dodgy circuitry in the electrics. Things which were a bigger challenge to him than fishing. So I collected the tackle and wandered down to the jetty by myself. It was a misty day, the fog shrouded the bay and smothered sound almost completely. When you stood next to the water, voices travelled over the top of it like sonar blips, trapped by the thick cloud of vapour. I walked out onto the jetty with yesterday's bait in the bucket. Without Dad I had lost the confidence and the will to go and collect fresh bait, and besides, the tide was up already. Standing at the end of the wall I dropped the bait over into the water and waited. The mist was so thick that I could barely see the foot of the jetty back by the beach. I was becalmed on a boat of stone.

The coalfish seemed to be encouraged by the ambient glow that pressed down upon them. From the first cast they bit with a ferocity I hadn't felt before and I soon had a bag full. I looked at my watch. It was about eleven. The mist had grown into a fog and I was beginning to feel more and more disorientated. Voices had raced across the sea all morning like a ceaseless gallery of whispers. As I couldn't see where they were coming from, they had a spooky edge, although they were probably just from the villagers collecting their groceries or newspapers, going about their business and greeting each other in the time-honoured fashion of a lazy Sunday. But sound without a picture had its own form and I soon began to feel restless. Suddenly, a bell tolled. Its peal was muffled at first but then it rolled across the water like a giant ball-bearing, growing in size until it seemed to split the atoms that were left in the thin air around me. My heart jumped and I waited for a second one. They came in quick succession and I imagined a ship, almost crewless and mastless, drifting across the empty bay whilst its brass bell rang telling all of the horrors it had witnessed.

I was transfixed. The ringing stopped. Voices again. Chasing themselves across the water in a frenzied cackle. And then they stopped too, and there was a momentary silence. I had reeled in and had not baited up for over ten minutes and my breath was so short the ether threatened to absorb me and leave my rod and reel as the only evidence I had been here at all. Then there was another voice. It spoke slowly, with an authority. It belonged to a priest. I was an avid anti-churchgoer at the best of times; mass seemed designed solely to cap a day already blessed with the mantle of boredom, Sunday. Perhaps my father's intuition had told him to stay away and this was his revenge on me for moaning about having to go to church every week. Here I was, a captive congregation, a rabbit in God's headlights, as the words of the service rolled out and the responses followed them unquestioningly.

It didn't once strike me as odd that the service was carrying on outside; in fact, the concept of outside had vanished as the layers of sea mist intensified. Perhaps the clouds had stolen the walls and roof of the church, perhaps there was a ship after all, mutinied, drifting with its remaining crew, the parched and the poxed sailors throwing their trust to the ship's parson in a blind hope that he would lead them ashore. As I pictured this the sermon began. The voice was more intense, faster and more searching than before, spelling out the weekly message in a precise hammer-like rhythm. It preached that there should be no labour on the day of the Sabbath. No washing, no cooking, no work of any kind. To do so was an affront to the laws of God. Normally, during the sermon back at home I would think about what I was going to have for lunch or wonder what was on television later that day. I knew what I would be having for lunch on this day – the same as yesterday and the day before: battered coalfish with Lea & Perrins, a couple of slices of bread and a cup of tea. But my appetite refused to kick-start. The suburbs, their safety, their predictability and many redundant Sundays spent in church suddenly seemed a very long way away. The rhythm of the sermon had risen and it was now like a manic chant. 'No work of any kind . . .'

I'm not sure if it was the voice or the summer sun but the white layers that sat on the water now began to clear with each word. I had had my back to the voice up until now but as the edges of the land came into sight I turned around to face it. Through a wispy veil of dancing mist I could make out the shape of a tower. Beneath it stood a crowd of fifty, maybe sixty people, static and motionless, staring, entranced by a tiny head which bobbed up and down and swung from side to side. With the lifting of the fog the voice started to fill the bay, booming out with all the vitriol of an insane dictator, 'And there shall be no work, and fires of hell shall consume those who choose to defy the teachings of the Bible.' He was raving. Completely rabid. And he was coming for us, I was sure of it; me for daring to fish in the sea on the day of rest and my father for having the nerve to repair his holiday cottage in sight of the big man. My mind raced and I wished I could swap my hooks and line for a set of rosary beads. The crowd were still static but had turned to look out across the bay and from behind them the spitting voice of the priest castigated the young fisherman on the stone jetty. I readied myself to be lynched and fed to the petrels.

I was so alarmed that I did not hear him approaching. He tapped my shoulder and I must have jumped a thousand feet. He laughed and asked whatever could be the matter? I'd closed my eyes in terror and on opening them fully expected to see Saint Peter with his keys in one hand and a list of excuses in the other. But it was my father. He'd come down to tell me it was lunchtime. He could tell that I was nervous and he asked why my fishing rod was on the floor of the jetty and not in my hand. I hastily tried to explain the mounting fear, the fog and the words that had come across the bay. Dad laughed it off, as he was wont to do with most things, particularly if there was a priest involved. A sort of derisory laugh, at once dismissive. 'Wouldn't worry about priests,' he said with a sticks-and-stones certainty. And this from the man who'd spent the first ten years of my life avoiding church until it was absolutely necessary to show a bit of willing in front of the collection plate. 'Come on, son, let's get some grub and come back later.' He was right, as usual, and it was soon forgotten as we gathered the stuff and walked back up the hill together towards the cottage, the hot sun on our backs and an empty village square behind us.

My father and religion. A book in itself. I knew the dogma of faith only too well. It was that which had shut the door so firmly on any sense of family from his side beyond his father and mother. I'd been born too late to meet my paternal grandmother and my grandfather had died four years earlier. I had vague memories of him in the house he lived in, always slipping me bottles of Coke and moving around the place slowly. The house there was old, its rooms dark and beyond the salvation of central heating. My brother lives in a house not dissimilar to that now and only had central heating fitted last year. Prior to that, he lived in the middle of the country in his old farmhouse, the winters giving out bronchial infections like bus tickets. He had lived with my grandfather as a child on many an occasion when my parents were abroad on new postings. I never thought about it until now but perhaps his refusal to install this most basic of modern comforts was a subconscious retreat to those inevitably idyllic days he would have spent in that Hampshire village of Liss.

My father, a Catholic with Irish parents, became a British soldier like his father and grandfather before him. In 1974 Dad came home one night and announced that for the time being there were to be no more pub lunches, or quick halves on the way back from visiting relatives. To reiterate the point he had a can of Watney's Party Seven under his arm and three or four bottles of Courage Pale Ale in his hand, which were stowed in the pantry and were to gather dust there for years. This followed the army pub ban after the bombings in Birmingham and Guildford. Dad was not a big pub-goer but I knew he found a sense of peace in them when he needed a breather or there was something serious to discuss. Pints of bitter and pork pies. My brother has his aversion to central heating and every now and again when I step into a pub I have this weird desire to order a bitter, maybe for Dad, because for him there was a time when he couldn't. He must have felt as if his past had really caught up with him then. He'd dropped the Kevin from his name and was known as

Ted. Saint Kevin, the patron saint of pursuit. An empty pint glass in one hand and a broken family tree in the other.

We returned to the jetty much later that day, after a trip to the castle at Portree. The tide had turned and was filling up the bay. The sunshine of earlier had given way to a sticky, dank and humid evening. As we walked along the jetty the air was full of midges, who seemed to be hatching incessantly, like amoebas, forming black, arabesque curtains every few yards. Just to walk through them to the end of the wall felt like a struggle. As if we weren't meant to fish at all.

Our bait was running low, was over a day old and had begun to take on a brackish smell. But we had neglected to collect anything fresh in the afternoon so it would have to do. The shanks of the hooks were a brilliant silver in the approaching twilight. The ageing orange mussel hearts were hard to impale but after a while we got the hang of it and our baits were in the water. To drive the midges away, my father lit his pipe and stood puffing on it like a sentry waiting for an armada. The evening was absolutely perfect for fishing. I felt certain we would catch fish immediately. But as is the case so often when you get this feeling, nothing happened for a good half an hour or so. The tide continued to rise up the wall, creeping up the bright-green algae-covered stones.

Dad tapped his pipe out on the heel of his shoe and I rebaited. Our fishing had reached the point where conversation had slipped away and been replaced by a mutual silence of satisfaction. We were together but alone with our thoughts. I stared down into the water, willing a bite to happen. Where had the coalfish gone? Had I fished them out earlier in the day and in doing so angered old Neptune himself? There was no way he was a Presbyterian, surely he didn't hold out with the ideals of no labour on a Sunday, too? I was off, imagining the Orange Marches being led by a grey bearded figure carrying a long fork, topped off with a bowler hat and a sash. I was brought back to my senses by a bite. Awake suddenly, I struck and felt a solid resistance. And then deep in the water there was movement. I could make out the faintest of shapes. Bigger than the coalfish. It refused to come to the surface for what seemed like minutes but was probably only seconds. When it did I winched it up the wall and onto the stones. A fish of about two pounds in weight. A mass of mottled brick-red and white spots with a giant's eye and a long whisker that ran off its chin. A cod. Its mouth was disproportionately big for its body. Wide and cavernous like the net of a trawler. I listened while Dad told me that it was not uncommon for trawler crews to gut cod and find empty beer cans from around the world rusting away in their stomachs. The cod had learnt that sea snails and the like would make a home inside the cans and so a small Skol or Worthington's E was like a ready meal in itself, the stomach acid rotting the thin aluminium away in days and giving its delicacies up like a tin pasty.

But I wasn't listening fully. To me, this fish was a renewal of faith. A defiant confirmation that I wasn't to be cursed for working on the day of rest. In fact, it implied completely the opposite. A bigger fish than usual, one which, back then, deserved a plate of chips and nothing less. It was holy, as if sent from the mount itself to feed us for a thousand meals, blessed with the incense of my father's Whiskey Flake tobacco. I looked across the bay at the church. Its doors were locked, the crowd had dispersed and the priest was long gone. It had lost all its semi-demonic aura of earlier, and was now just another building on the waterfront amongst the scattering of houses and the post office.

I baited up quickly and insisted that Dad did the same. There had to be more than one down there. Our conversation perked up with our expectation and then fell silent again moments later. The lines were still. The dusk was coming on. I was sure I could make out a rumble of thunder in the distance, but it was hard to tell. The night closed in on us with a lonely oppression. Even though we stood side by side, I still felt that magical isolation and, soon, the realisation that it was time to head for the yellow lights of our cottage up the hill. When we could almost see no more we lifted our lines out of the water. I could make out the fluorescent glow of my bait as the hook swung in. Dad was still pulling his line up but there was a resistance on the end. In the dark we peered over the wall to see what would break the surface. We could hear the splash but not see the shape or form of a fish. Within seconds it was at our feet. I crouched down to pick it up and let out a cry. It was an eel, its back fully spined. I cut my fingers on it. Dad stood on it with his shoe, reached down, parted the line with his teeth and kicked it over the wall and into the sea. I had no idea what kind of species it was, or where it had come from. It was like a micro-dinosaur, a palaeolithic oddity. In my mind, even now, I can make out the yellow of its eye, vivid even in the dark, the serpent as messenger, venomously mocking me for having the front to think that good could exist without evil.

Chapter Two

It was 1999, midsummer – or as close as it comes to it on the east coast. I pulled the car through the lanes of Suffolk, past primeval forest and acres of ripe corn that crowned the thin earth in quiet contrast to the broken oaks and skeletal elms. There were no road signs, nor were there any road markings. The sides of the lanes were lipped with a sand that washed away under the box hedge, and across the fields. To the west the evening sun tilted in through the windscreen and blinded me round each corner. To the east the light from the setting sun lit up the dying sky, gold on blue, with a vivid turquoise band giving away the presence of the sea. I drove towards it, the pull almost magnetic, waiting for the fields to fall away and open up to the water beyond. I was going fishing for bass.

Known as the silver wolf of the sea, the bass migrates up from the Mediterranean in the warmer months and is as much a token of summer on English beaches as the cod is of winter. It thrives off the west coast of Ireland, where the Gulf Stream flows between veins of land and the Atlantic roar blesses the sandy bays with surf. In recent years it seems to have become a stranger to our shores, despite the rise in water temperature, and due to its fashionable status is hunted not only by the angler but by the dark hulk of the factory ship. Every fishmonger in London sells bass undersize, some no larger than a herring. Demand has turned the wolf of the sea into an angel of the table. I sought it as my own guardian: a couple of pounds of hope, a messenger from beyond the seventh wave.

I fished the beach first. I tackled up with an old Edgar Sealey beach caster, twinned with an Intrepid Surfcaster reel. I bound a peeler crab round the shank of the hook with an elasticated thread. The thread cut into the shell of the crab and cocooned its legs. I scrambled across the stones and, swinging the line in a pendulum action, hurled the offering out past the end of the groines until I could see the distant splash of the lead on the water. I sat and waited. The beach curved away in a terrace to my left towards the faint edge of Aldeburgh town. Behind the sea defences, the shallow and brackish waters of the River Alde crept disconcertingly across the flood flats. Curlews called, an ageless shrill, midges danced, hatching in their hundreds as dusk came, attendants to a fading evening in an old Victorian English resort. I was fishing the 'dirty wall', but tonight it defied both its name and the anger of the North Sea. It was simply a place at peace with itself; the tide so lazy, it could not find the energy to lap against the shore. A giant asleep.

———•———

The ward was full but there was no doctor to be seen. In the beds lay people propped up by pillows and chemicals, dripped out to oblivion. The stench of disinfectant was cooked by the heat, which, even in May, pumped out of the radiators along the side of the wall. The windows were shut tight and televisions crackled and hissed as their receptions cut in and out. The floor was polished and squeaky under foot. It was as if someone had decided that cleanliness alone was enough to fight off disease. Sets of eyes watched me and I looked back. The ones I was searching for were not amongst them. But this was his ward, this was where he was meant to be. I walked on, to the next one, where the scene was the same without relent. At the end of the corridor was a door, with a strip of glass built into it. I approached it and peered in. Through the grid of wire I saw the face of my father, with its usual smile both on the mouth and in the eyes. No wonder he wasn't on the ward. Too soon for that, or perhaps a question of never. My heart leapt. Relief lifted my frame. The door had been opened already. My mother was in there, helping my father off his bed.

It had been a small tumour. The size of an old ten pence piece. Masked by a nipple. Quietly growing deep in his lung, undetected by the six-monthly check that the throat cancer had necessitated ten years before. After years of a clear chest it seemed that he had escaped. Given up just in time. And then the nipple grew until it was bigger than the other. A simple operation was all it needed. A removal, only of the lump, not the lung itself. So abstract, so easy. There was still no doctor there. They'd left their mark, though. A scar reached across Dad's back from hip to shoulder like a sash. Freshly stitched and dressed in cotton and sterile tape. There was a conversation, but I couldn't take it in; the scar seemed so out of proportion with the diagnosis. As we helped him to the car I listened to the conversation as if it was going on between people I'd never met. They hadn't removed a thing. The growth had spread back from the lung into the lymph glands. Inoperable.

The giant had stayed asleep and though I'd fished well past sunset there were no silver bass on the silent tide. The sun had gone and the wind had picked up. I tried to shelter behind the patch of rocks beneath the wall but the cold ate at my neck and stiffened my back. After a while it seemed futile to cast. The stillness was like a cloak shutting out all life. I waited of course, becoming what every true angler is – a statue of time, halted. A flag of hope planted in the stones marking the very spot where others' patience is all but gone. Waiting for a flicker of life, an assurance that beneath the surface of the water is a shape, searching through the green and grey shades of half-light for a trussed-up meal, nailed to the floor of the sea by a four-ounce lead and buoyed up by a plastic bead.

As the headlights lit the locked boatyard and the heater blew a stale fug through the car, I shivered and swore. I could only think of tea and sleep but in my heart I knew I'd be back at the wall tomorrow to fish the down tide in search of red gills and their gospel. It is the same whenever the bass don't come. I notice the air around me, how it closes in and pushes me ever closer to the water. With a fish caught the sky is like a cathedral, all choirs and celebration, all stained glass and worship – of nature, of being alive. Without, the same open

sky is like a crypt, the clinging damp and the dark
incessantly sad, imploring you to get back up to London,
past the circling headlamps on the roundabouts, the next-
door cars with hangers in the back and vacant drivers in the
front, dodging the Spanish lorries with '70s graphics and
glowing virgins blinking on the dash, to find your space in
the lane.

Once I had been a stranger to the motorway, after May of
'91, as the shock sank in and I shied from the truth. It was
another summer, the last chance of youthful oblivion and
carefree existence. I burnt like a Catherine wheel, splendid
and wounded, careering across the long months, a compass
without points. He was having chemotherapy, his sickness
rife and debilitating, the fear becoming real. And perhaps it
was for me, too, as I drank and fought, shaved my head and
hardened to the world. Warehouses, cellars, sound systems,
clubs, watching the sun rise off the Thames, seeking all the
time to find the furthest place from it all. My job sent me
round the country. Sheffield, Aberdeen, Newcastle. The
anonymity of the hotel and the open bar suiting me just fine.
But by Christmas it was already too late. No more chemo. It
was pointless they said. A waste of time. The family
gathered ceremoniously for lunch, dressed in paper hats and
wearing fragile smiles. We ate and we drank and a silent clock
ticked over the table.

I did not fish at this time. I hadn't fished since I was fifteen.
I'd left it behind in the escape from my childhood. Locked my
rods and reels up amongst boxes in the garage and agreed that,
yes, it was a good idea to sell them once I'd left home. They
only cluttered the place up. I passed places on the train

journeys down from London where Dad and I had fished together. It seemed as if everyone had left, years before, when I had. There was never anyone fishing. Empty banks, the swims dwarfed by willows, and the poplars on the far side being stripped of the last of their leaves in the winter winds. I stood in the doorway between two lives. I remembered so clearly that day when Dad had returned home from work, whistling, cheerful (was he ever any other way?). In his hand was a brown paper bag. He spilled the contents onto the table as we had our tea. There was a yellow card, folded in two, with a strip of paper glued onto the inside leaf. On this was written our name and address. On the front was a block print of a castle, the date 1912, and the words 'Farnham Angling Society'. It was our permit. Membership for father and son. And now, looking back, how I would love to have taken him out for one last trip. A walk together along the winter river, a crisp blue morning by a still lake. But these were not the feelings I had at the time of his illness. I did all I could to anaesthetise myself from any feelings at all. I suppose we were all under siege. Each one coping. Him, the stoic, us the support. Never alone, bound together by humour and small kindnesses, keeping face, soldiering on.

———

It was the next day. Overnight the wind had picked up. A strong easterly. The sun shone and clouds like Constable's own skitted across the sky, their edges lit like sulphur, chasing one another from town to town. The sea was different. Bright green in the glare, visibility nil, arms and legs of weed torn up and thrown to the surface. Breakers rolling and crashing; the shingle awash and gleaming, a glorious noise, fresh and full of life. The skin tightened on my face in the salty, dry air. There would have to be a bass. Beyond the sixth, or maybe the seventh, rolling in on the tide, chasing sand eel, in packs of three and four. Shoals of eyes and spines, alive and hunting. I reached for my bait. The sea water in the bucket was going stale in the sun. The crabs climbed on each other's backs and scrambled up the sides before slipping back down. A writhing mass of claws and horns. I picked one out. Its pincers nipped and clung onto my fingers. The scissors broke its neck. I peeled the shell from its back and trussed the claws. Another one and the rig was ready. I climbed into the waves and laughed as their momentum lifted my feet, picked me up, and set me down. The pendulum swung and the lead and line took the bait far out.

The beach was getting fuller. A Sunday afternoon. Cars went up and down the makeshift road between the beach and the marsh. Couples sat in parked cars, glasses to the horizon, with their coats on and the windows up, some asleep with heads back and mouths open. Fathers with their children and dogs ran along the beach, dodging the waves, shrieking every now and again as the water caught them. There were just a few other fishermen, much further down the beach, their distant forms shimmering in the haze. Every now and again I could hear the sound of voices from a mile away. An opera was being broadcast through a loudspeaker in Aldeburgh. It was the story of Peter Grimes, the Britten fisherman who became outlawed, an enemy of the people, marginalised, demonised, driven to his death off the shallow cliffs. His pleading had been carried on the wind and the witch hunt chant of the chorus pursued him, hundreds of years later, but no less determined. The tide had risen and pushed me until I could go no further; I was backed up against the wall. My baits stayed untouched, passed over for another afternoon, the fish absent in protest. I'd spoken to no one for hours, but it felt so much longer than that. I threw the rest of the peelers to the birds and washed the bucket out. My hands stank and I longed to go home.

Going home. Something I'd done by chance one January weekend long ago. He lay propped up in my bed, a giant oxygen bottle standing next to him like an aqualung prepared for a long dive. It was shell grey, with a fitted brass top and a glass-faced dial on the front. A needle lay still to the left, out of the black, out of the red, waiting to measure out each breath. From a tap, an orange rubber pipe led to a mask, plastic and seemingly inadequate next to the engineering of the tank. Everything was out of kilter, not in balance. I'd just popped in, for a cup of tea, en route to nowhere, perhaps en route to knowing. There was a mild panic in the rooms of the house. The sickness seemed intent on hunting us all down. It was out now, it had won and was beating at the windows and rattling the doors in triumph, laughing last as it always seems to do. He lay propped up in bed, his eyes still smiling and his chest watery, but pushing up on his elbows, always, always, 'Hello, son.' The handshake was still strong and certain. Improbably it gave out hope, as if the atmosphere was all wrong, it was alright, it was okay. On a shelf next to the bed were collections of old photographs, the kind that get relegated to a spare room when it's been vacated. In one a younger me smiled up at the camera, fish at my feet, on the steps of a cottage in Skye. It was already another lifetime away. My eyes passed over it without a second thought, certain that it was only forwards now, there would be no looking back, no reminiscing, no nostalgia, no compassion. A heart hardened and a mind definite, intent, staring out to the horizon, looking for shapes and pillars of smoke.

Over that day and into the evening all the family gathered around my mother as she nursed Dad. It became apparent that I hadn't really known the extent of the decline that they had gone through the past weeks alone together. We'd waited by phones and pressed on. There'd been a night when they thought it was going to happen, a week and a half or so earlier, and my brother had driven out in the night, to go through all the papers. Checking that the hatches were battened down. Ready for the final push. I remember my sister, Gill, collapsing on the doorstep around seven, a tiny fury of anxiety, terrified that she hadn't made it in time. My father's brother and his wife came and made sandwiches. Ham and cheese. Platefuls. And there was tea of course. We all talked and cajoled, restless and waiting. I took Dad for a walk. Not by the river or by the lake, but across the pages of a book, one of the many that lay next to his bed – gifts, all of them, parcels of morale. Amongst them was one I'd originally intended for his birthday the following March but had given him for Christmas in another subconscious moment of knowing. It was *Islands in the Stream* by Hemingway. Perhaps I had felt that Dad needed the strength of another man in exile; someone else a long way from home who ate and drank life for its own sake. It lay unthumbed, spine out, as it still does now, years later. I must have written a dedication in the front. I could not look at it. I read from something else that day, a book about a different soldier who'd fought battles many miles away from this small suburban room. Dad listened as I read the words out. I was conscious of my voice, growing louder, as the words echoed, bouncing off the walls and drowning out the sound of passing cars. In the evening, we opened a bottle of wine and drank together. The glass still seemed so small, cupped in his hands, his large knuckles guarding it, his skin a map, knitted with brown pigment, reminders of the sun. He slept.

G and I left London early. The curtains were still drawn and there was dew on the rooftops, the smell of a city dawn festering in the small streets. We drove out across the Essex marshland, past the Tarkovskian GPO building near Ipswich and onto Dunwich. By the time we'd arrived the sun had gone and in the wind you could hear the mythical church bell ringing in the waves. We climbed down onto the beach, past the fragile sandy cliffs, collapsing winter on winter into the sea but pocked in spring with the nests of swifts. The surf fizzed and a spray of mist stretched out either side of us into nothing. To my right, floating, hallucinogenic, like a sterile honeycomb, was the nuclear power station Sizewell B. It was still relatively early in the year for the bass, but if they were anywhere on this coastline it would be here, where the outflow from the cooling systems heated the sea and defied the charts.

There was a duel going on here – between Sizewell, where nurture and all its scientific wonder staked its authority, and Dunwich, where nature clawed that old arrogance back to into her lap. We tried to fish but as the morning went on, the sea rose and an anger crashed down on the softness of the early haze. The swell battered the sand and standing in the surf became impossible.

———•———

Dad made it through the night. There was a strange sense that he shouldn't have. It was enough to hint at a reprieve. *The sea was different. Bright green in the glare, visibility nil, arms and legs of weed torn up and thrown to the surface.* The doctor came, and with him, the smell of the outside world. There was a fresh coldness on his coat, morphine in his pocket. Someone had turned up the radiators and closed the windows. We did things but talked little. I walked around in a daze. My mind is still blank years on. There was waiting, a lot of waiting. *I tried to shelter behind the patch of rocks beneath the wall but the cold ate through my neck and stiffened my back.* There was a lot of discussion, should the priest see him or not? He was from Belfast. In between masses. Dad didn't need that kind of reminder on this day. His last. Normally he wouldn't give him house room and, now, here came the church, all incense and glory, gathering another lamb in the valley so dark. Belfast or not, the past or not, a prayer was a prayer, so the priest knelt, with us half in and half out of the room. *A flag of hope planted in the stones marking the very spot where others' patience is all but gone.* Dad moved and struggled in and out of consciousness. I lifted his tongue and underneath was the orange dot of morphine, unswallowed. We washed it down. His hand could not hold the glass so well now. It was as if overnight the life had shrunk away from him. It was that fast. The priest had gone and we all gathered in the small room. All together. The silent clock grew louder and ticked towards one. There was confusion and then silence. *We tried to fish but as the morning went on the sea rose and an anger crashed down on the softness of the early haze. The swell battered the sand and standing in the surf became impossible.*

———

In the year of our Lord 1180, near Orford in Suffolk, there was a fish taken in the perfect shape of a man; he was kept by Bartholomew de Glanville in the Castle of Orford above half a year; but at length not being carefully looked to, he stole to the sea and was never seen after. He never spake, but would eat any meat that was given him, especially raw fish, when he had squeezed out the juice: He was had to church, but never shewed any signe of adoration.

The Gentleman's Recreation, Nicholas Cox, 1674

———

The marshland was flat and dirty, the wind chasing the grass incessantly, trying to drown it in the putrid bogs that made up the landscape. G and I stood in the car park, an indeterminate patch of broken tarmac that had marooned itself behind the sea wall. To our right the river churned out to the sea down a concrete-lined canal, whose walls were green with damp and black with silt. Clouds sat like a stone coffin lid above all of this and the air was thick with salt. It felt hard to breathe.

The roar where the pipe from the channel met the incoming sea grew louder. I looked over towards it. The tide was rampant and the waves just kept coming, a filthy brown, the colour of cold tea and no less enticing. To fish in these conditions, in this place, especially for the bass, seemed impossible. It seemed as if the sea were empty, its bed interspersed with clutches of long strangling weed, stretching up through the gloom, washing this way and that with each tide, its sullen moan asking the same question, over and over again. Where had all the fish gone?

And so it seemed on land. The landscape before me was a mirror of the one under the waves. Just as bare and empty, with the same choking lack of an essential oxygen or life force. What was a bass after all? It had become an almost holy creature, whose shoals once lit the seas with a symphony of ease and grace. To most it was a badge, but to me something much, much more personal. I found myself stopping at stories in the paper. Of the disappearing cod, fished from existence for a society wasted on abundance. Of the coelacanth, once assumed to be a prehistoric remnant, fossilised in history, now thought to be swimming in the warm seas off Africa. Of the sprat, relegated to a nursery rhyme and now raining down on the roofs of Thorpeness in freak weather. There were no stories of bass though. It seemed that it did not belong in any popular folklore, but this fish and certain others were like phantoms to me, each one haunting me with their own character and tale, each one coaxing me with another part of a message.

As I pursued them, sleep became less of a night's certainty and more of a day-long wish. The things I saw and the places I went to began to possess me more and more. When I was at home all I could think of was being out there and when I was there I was often completely alarmed and could only think of pavements, streetlamps and a sense of security long disrupted.

I looked round and G was busy striking a deal with a couple of blokes who'd parked up next to us in a rusty old Toyota. Inside the car the plastic seat covers had deteriorated and foam poked through. Fat spots of rain landed on the roof. Under the raised lid of the boot was an old orange chip-fat bucket, and inside this was a writhing mass of peeler crab – hundreds of them, the sound of their scratching claws cracking in whispers. Their pedlars were men beyond time. Gaunt faces, the colour drained out, deep lines covering skin grey with nicotine. Days' worth of growth lined their mouths, and matted greasy hair poked out from under faded baseball caps. In the gloom though, their eyes were sharp, never still, darting between G and I. They had no time to waste. One of them drew on a cigarette, the tip fizzing in the rain, coughed and then spat into a puddle at our feet. G handed over a tenner. The spitter tipped up the bucket and the flailing crabs fell in a spindle into our open bag. The boot was slammed, bags were gathered and the pair set off. Off and out. To a place well out beyond the point where the mouth of the river roared out from the concrete confines of the estuary canal and into the sea. I could no longer tell whether they were an apparition or not. I watched as their figures turned into black specks on the horizon. With them went everything I was after. A time, unknown; a place, off the map; an identity, abandoned – and most importantly of all an answer, to why I had started to fish again. There was something in between the idyll of Skye and its portents, and these new empty-handed days on the seashore where I seemed to be surrounded by unlikely crusaders and ghosts in the form of fish. When had it all started? I had to go back and retrace the steps, see if they fell into any kind of rhythm. Until then I would be like a hymn without a number.

Chapter Three

It had all started one night outside the Lansdowne pub on Gloucester Avenue, Chalk Farm, north London. I was working round the corner in the new offices of Creation Records, which at the time was on the verge of national notoriety. Everyone at the office had populated the closest pub to our building on Regent's Park Road, the infamous Pembroke Castle. It was once quite a sad old boozer and then Creation arrived and its profits went through the roof. I was a withdrawn, almost conscientious objector to the incessant partying that you could always find if you looked, and as a result I tended to avoid the Pembroke when I could and frequented the Lansdowne.

It was a summer evening, one of those when London is almost fragrant and the whole world seems to have spilled out onto the pavement, pints in hand, to fill the streets with voice and laughter. I'd gone to have a meal with my wife, Deborah, and we were due to meet up with her brother, Oliver. As usual Oliver turned up late with his boss in tow, G, an old friend of Deborah's. He was straight out of *The Guardian*'s *Space* magazine, even if he didn't see it that way. G ran (and still does, despite fantasies to give it all up for an Airstream and a Colt 45) a very hip architecture practice. His whole existence seemed to be one massive lifestyle spread. He'd just returned from three weeks on the Suffolk coast, where he'd stayed with his girlfriend and their two kids in an artist's studio. I listened in envy and awe as G explained to me his daily ritual. At about five in the evening, given a good tide, he would leave the cottage and amble down to the beach where he would fish in the surf for bass. With each tide he could be guaranteed at least three or four good fish. In the dying light he'd string them up by the gills and wander back to the cottage, dinner sorted. It was not long before we were both eulogising about the joys of fishing and I was picturing the idyllic existence he'd had over the past three weeks. With every Guinness I was unlocking thoughts which had lain dormant for years. I hadn't fished since I was fifteen. Here I was aged twenty-nine, recently married, in a mad job, ensconced in London. Why did I have this sudden urge to fish that very evening?

By last orders the sky had faded from turquoise to dark blue and for once I had noticed it – a sure sign that I was weather watching. Even now I can't get into the car without checking the air temperature on the dashboard and weighing up the conditions whilst I turn over the ignition. D says this is one of the new habits which I have developed since getting back into the angle. That and phoning the ten-day long-range forecast when she's not in the room.

As G and I talked one thing was absolutely for certain. I had to go fishing – and soon. There I was, nearly fifteen years on the angling wagon, and one conversation had pushed me off. That's how it seemed that evening, as we talked about trout in the Scottish Isles, bass and whiting off the beach, and pike lurking in the black bomb craters of our collective childhoods. Drunken plans were made, phone numbers exchanged and pledges made to go fishing as soon as possible. I had no gear, had not wet a line in anger for over a decade and had no wheels either – but these were not barriers, as I was getting into something that defied the practical and owed everything to dreams. As with all those conversations, the life-affirming ones which develop special meaning after six pints, absolutely no action followed. I was soon back into the routine of working during the week and trekking off to festivals to take my place in the hospitality bar for the rest of the summer. I didn't even meet up with G again until just after Christmas when Deborah and I went round for supper. He and K had just returned from a holiday in the Caribbean at Ian Fleming's old retreat. We didn't talk about fishing until the very end of the evening when our idea to go was resurrected. A date was set: we'd go on the last day of the current coarse season, 14 March – it might have seemed a long way away but in our career-laden lives if you didn't book months upfront, things would materialise and fill the time.

That was the easy bit, all we had to do now was justify what we were doing – to our families, our friends and to each other. This was London 1996, on the brink of the birth of the 'new lad'. Maybe there was a chance that we could do it and get away with it. If people questioned it we could just say, 'Yeah, fishing, like *The Deer Hunter* but without Meryl Streep or the Vietnam bit.'

I was sure that this would do the trick and so it was that we started to transform ourselves into a budding de Niro and Walken, intent on getting out into the hills. For weeks at work I found myself drifting off into the dialogue of that film – and into another, older dialogue, one I hadn't had for years. I had by now ceased to cry when I thought of my father; meeting D had purged me of my grief and we lived lives of optimism and joy. I smiled a lot, laughed even more, and was convinced I'd freed myself from the shadows. But since making our date to go fishing I had started to recall things.

The first sign was when we went down to visit my mum. Before she'd finished telling me her news on arrival, I'd picked up a set of keys, opened the back door and headed off in the direction of the shed. The musty smell of old creosote filled my head as I started to root around for my old fishing tackle. A lump formed in my throat as I stopped and looked around at all the old tools above the workbench. I felt like one of those divers who swims through a porthole of a sunken ship and sifts through the crockery, silver and sand. I was not alone, a spirit filled that small space and I was disturbing it. I fully expected my dad's sawn-off wellingtons to walk out from under the bench and set off in search of the lawnmower. I took a few deep breaths and locked the door behind me. On another visit to Mum I ended up with four carrier bags full of fishing books which I'd liberated from the shelves in my old room. My bed was still there, made up, undisturbed, and with the spirit not far away. On the shelf a younger me smiled back, sitting on the steps of a Scottish cottage with fish at my feet. It made me think that there must be dozens of similar photos hidden away in the house. I had a sudden desire to root them out and wade through them. It's not easy to do; it seems so impolite to ignore the living and go off looking for a token of the past, so I had to be discreet. There was an old suitcase which was packed with them – years' and years' worth of moments. Among them I found a black-and-white, four-by-four, white-bordered print. I would have ignored it normally and carried on looking for a face I knew, for some kind of confirmation that there had been a 'before'. But it became a treasured possession. In the picture I'm sitting next to my father and I'm holding a fishing rod.

The morning of my trip with G soon came around. I had felt the same trepidation the evening before that I had often felt as a child before going fishing. An excitement takes over and you are unable to concentrate on small things that you'd normally do without thinking. G was driving as I was still without a car at that time and he'd arranged to pick me up at 7 a.m. We were going to a place called Old Bury Hill Lake near Dorking in Surrey. It was a weekday. We were both so awkward and reticent about going that the idea that we'd go when there wouldn't be other anglers around to cast aspersions over our technique or approach seemed the only option. It also gave the venture a subversive flavour: the very beginnings of opting out of the rat race. This added symbolism to our day out and justified it, which was more important than anything else. This is a feeling which still persists today.

It was still dark when the buzzer sounded. What was I doing out of bed voluntarily before sunrise? Was I completely mad? I laugh about the fact now but all I took with me that morning was a coat and an old pair of boots. This was a sure sign that I was still in denial. G had all the gear, it was stuffed into the back of his Golf, buried under the baby seats. I knew something was up as soon as I was in the car as the bags had a khaki tinge to them. I couldn't hold off the fact now – I was about to go fishing again.

We hit the south circular and within minutes had ground to a halt. Despite leaving at this ungodly hour we'd hit the rush hour. This suited me just fine at the time though, as things were going a little too fast anyway. Somewhere off the A3 we stopped for breakfast at a truckers' café, which served us sweet milky tea and bacon sandwiches. Half an hour later we pulled into the car park at Old Bury Hill. In the semi-darkness we unloaded the contents of the car and walked off to the booking office. It was a wooden structure built on stilts at the edge of the lake. It was fully kitted out in an American survival style: billets, tables, a kitchen for fry-ups and had a small tackle shop selling live bait and bits of tackle. We bought a couple of day tickets from the weary owner who took us round to the boathouse. The banks of the lake were a quagmire so it only seemed reasonable to resort to taking a punt, of which there were several tied up. Moments later we were casting off and moving away stealthily. The layer of cloud which had greeted us at first light was beginning to clear as a weak sun eased through it and the lake began to steam. The fresh air hit as we rowed across the lake towards an island that the bloke in the hut had assured us was our only chance of a place to catch anything that day. Prising myself out of bed in the cold and dark; traffic jams; endless days in the office; late nights driving back from gigs in Norwich or Manchester and sitting bug-eyed in my kitchen at 4 a.m. – all these things seemed to be lifted from me with each stroke of the oar. The sunlight was truly golden. The escape had begun. We were over the fence and running.

We dropped anchor behind the island which was a maze of rhododendron bushes. Amongst the roots of these lurked pike of gargantuan proportions and the exotic zander. When I was a child the zander had a demonic quality. Occasionally, you would see rare photographs of it in fishing newspapers. A large black-and-golden eye sat above a toothy shark-like jaw. Its skin was a shroud of spiny scales which gave off a metallic-blue tint. Astride of this was a majestic dorsal sail fin with huge spines protruding out of it. This was the original tin fish. It was not one of the indigenous species of our islands and could only be caught in places which were well off the beaten track, almost beyond civilisation, like the Fens or Woburn Abbey, where that other monster of dreams resides: the giant catfish or 'wels'. Originally stocked there, presumably by some mad aristocrat intent on creating a nineteenth-century neverland, the zander had migrated, carried by birds, from the lake at the Abbey to the Fenland drain system.

Have you ever been to the Fens? It is the one place left on our islands that modern society has failed to conquer. Vast, empty steel skies stretch across a completely flat and brutalised land. There are no trees. There are a few birds, picking away at the eroding fields like desperate famine survivors. In between all of this, flowing at a pace lower than a heartbeat, are drainage systems which allow the land to be farmed. You see the odd person behind the wheel of a tractor or a combine harvester but what you sense more than anything is that nature is cruel and that you are her unwelcome visitor. Given that the zander has thrived here one can only assume that it has a pact with a higher force. It is a behemoth, an underwater alien. When I was a child the prospect of catching such a fish seemed inconceivable – not because it was a rarity but simply because of the certain and comforting knowledge that there was no way you would be found in the places where they could be caught. The Fens were haunted open spaces best left alone to exorcists and outlaws. Not the place for a Catholic with a vivid imagination. Normal people lived in houses close to a station or a corner shop, had electricity and ate fish on a Friday. The people in the Fens had no station, the line stopped at Ely. They were known as Fen Tigers and they lived on eels and root vegetables. Here I was, years later, on a punt in a lake as the mist rose around us about to fish for that elusive zander.

For some unknown reason the fish had also been stocked in a few fisheries around the country, one in Yorkshire, one in Warwickshire and in Old Bury Hill Lake. It is reminiscent of the story of a German composer who spent his childhood locked away in a cellar before he was discovered at the age of twelve, a completely wild beast. Society did its best to tame him and make him respectable by dressing him in the clothes of the day and educating him. Tutelage and tea parties sent him only further over the edge, where he became a composer of beautiful music before killing himself in his twenties. Is this what someone had had in mind when they stocked those three rogue lakes with our native eastern European? An empirical campaign of domestication? A classic Edwardian or Victorian fantasy, carried out in secret by some pioneering naturalists?

Whatever had happened, the zander was reluctant to keep spreading and halted, like a migratory snapshot. We'd been told that the only time we'd be likely to catch one would be at dusk, and to do so we would have to fish under the roots of the bushes on the island. I sat spooked in the boat as G tackled up. He was using an old Bruce and Walker ledgering rod. Here we were about to fish for the oldest citizen of our waterways, the pike, and its new pretender from Bavaria, the zander, and G was going about it with some vintage English tackle. In addition to his rod G said I could use the split-cane B James of Ealing Richard Walker Mk IV Carp. This was a work of supreme craftsmanship, named after a pioneer of post-war angling, the legendary Richard Walker, himself a pied piper to every boy who had fished in the '60s and '70s. Reels were Garcia Mitchell 300s. Precision French engineering. Too expensive to even consider buying as a child, these were objects of design desire. For once I was grateful that G was an architect and a full-on style fascist. I felt like Edward Fox in *The Day of the Jackal*.

Threading the line through the rings of the Mark IV, I felt a sensation which I had not felt for a long time. A distinct sharpening of the heart and breath, a speeding sense of anticipation, a very real feeling of complete excitement. My hands shook as I tried to dredge from my mind the turns and tucks of a blood knot. Within seconds I had secured the wire trace necessary to blunt the teeth of our predators and was reaching into the bucket for a live roach or rudd. My first cast took over from my last one all those years ago. My reflexes woke up in the warm sun and fifteen years became fifteen minutes. The bright-orange float sat innocently under the shade of the bushes, waiting. The door which we'd opened had been temporarily shut on the world and we drifted to and fro in the punt, yawning and waiting. This is the popular vision of an angler: a dormant male who sits motionless on a riverbank and scowls at passers-by. There were no passers-by on this March morning. We'd guessed right – we were the only people fishing the lake. The trial of an early start had gifted us some solitude.

It seemed an eternity since I had felt sun gently creep across my bones and relax me. Where had I been for all those intervening years? In all that time, had I spent more than half an hour or an hour in the open air just sitting, other than when I'd been on holiday, stuck on a beach with all the other packaged holidaymakers anxious to get back to their routines? Had I ever in that time taken a boat out on a lake for longer than an hour? Here there was no loud hailer to call your number, to tell you that your time was up. Here you had a valid reason for staying well and truly put for the day. You could plot the progress of the sun as it staggered across the sky in anticipation of spring. You had the time to notice kingfishers flash across the green of the island and to see formations of Canadian geese flying far away, silhouetted against the pale sky. I could only liken it to meditation, a sort of waterborne yoga. Without knowing it, I had replaced fear of Fen with love of zen.

Conversation dropped to its natural male level, conspicuous anecdotes punctuated by grunts and nods. It was truly wonderful. I tried to think about what it was I would normally be doing at this time on a Tuesday. It was now about 12.30 p.m. and normally I would be sat hunched behind my desk at the offices of Creation. Anyone watching the rise of the label in the public eye that year could be forgiven for assuming that Creation Records was not a place of work but a palace of leisure. Did we not operate out of a Le Corbusian development in the heart of Soho? Was the office not staffed by a mixture of drug bunnies and superfly beats? Was there not a hotline to Central Office? Did meeting rooms not buzz with braced policymakers mapping out the charter for social change? You would think so if you read the papers, or watched the television, or listened to so-called popular radio in 1996. There was a revolution in attitudes afoot. Tired of platonic relationships and political correctness, the collective male of the nation had picked up his coat (a Stone Island cagoule, naturally) and walked.

A band on Creation called Oasis gave the social shift a sense of justification, and all of a sudden it was better to be arrogant than awkward. In turn the label earned a fortune off the back of the sales of the album *(What's the Story?) Morning Glory*. As Creation was a true independent (despite being 49 per cent owned by multinational Sony at the time) its income was not blown on flashy offices. We worked out of a converted chapel in the cosy but far from rock 'n' roll neighbourhood of Primrose Hill, north London. When I say converted chapel you are probably picturing stripped wooden floors, huge windows letting in the light and quiet phones purring gently on executive desks. What you should picture is your local cab office at 11.30 p.m. on a Friday night. Toilets and disused showers face you as you go through the door and you can't order a cab because the cramped room is too full to be productive – full of papers, full of posters and boxes, full of instruments, stray furniture and stray people. The controller is laughing manically at you from behind a pair of wraparound shades, and deep down you wish you were somewhere else. But you need to be there because it's the only realistic way home.

Day-to-day life at Creation was fun; it flew past in an uncontrollable manner. But nevertheless the reality was a tube journey, a desk, a phone, a computer, a fax and meeting after meeting about play lists, videos, production, artwork (the only redeeming factor), deadlines, scheduling, artists who didn't want success but who could attain it and artists who did want success but couldn't. It meant numerous nights away in Novotels in Frankfurt or Holiday Inns in Manchester wishing that licensing hours applied to hotels and laughing emptily as you were swiped for the remaining credit on your company card. It meant afternoons listening to opinions that were risible at best and contemptuous at worst. It meant days spent shaking your head in disbelief at the constant circus of indulgence that went on all around.

So what's wrong with that, I hear you say? It sounds absolutely wonderful. I check out in a supermarket; I work in insurance; I have a straight job in a dull industry. I would swap my job for that any day of the week. And you would. And you mightn't be a fool to do so either. You would have a ball – but at some point you would not be able to tell where the party ended and the hangover began. You would have walked into someone's hotel room (the door being ajar) at 10 a.m. on a weekday morning, with the curtains closed, the TV on with the sound turned down, the minibar empty, and vodka bottles strewn about. You'd be trying to wake up the fully clothed person in one of the twin beds because two hours earlier, having declared lifelong friendship, they had made you promise you'd put them on the same train as you in the morning. Or you would be standing in one of London's premier venues with a sticky carpet underfoot and a can of warming Red Stripe in your hand whilst someone you tolerated but despised gave you a lecture in your right ear about release dates or midweeks or cover-mounted CDs. Or you would be sitting indoors on a gloriously sunny Sunday afternoon waiting to hear news of a bad chart position, after which you are meant to feign disappointment on a par with grief, fake a breakdown and then phone twenty people in the hope of eliciting the same response in them.

So, as I say, normally at this time I would have been sitting behind my desk at Creation Records. It should have and could have been a paradise but it patently wasn't. It wasn't that I didn't enjoy my days or that I loathed and dreaded getting out of bed in the morning. It was more the fact that the timing was all wrong, which in retrospect was probably a very good thing. Nagging grief had burnt me out and I had partied long and hard enough to know that it wasn't me any more. But it hadn't even been me on the day that I joined Creation back in 1994. I'd come from the relatively organised and corporate environment of Virgin Retail. I'd been to management seminars, I'd been assessed, I'd been regraded, I'd been fast-tracked and sidelined. But I had got out and then found myself in a room in a ramshackle Victorian terrace off Mare Street in Hackney. My desk backed onto a railway line and trains shook the room every twenty minutes or so. I had a list of ten things to do in my first week. By lunchtime on my first day I'd done them all. They weren't real tasks as such, they were more welcoming gestures, designed to settle me in. I was asked to find a desk and a chair, order a computer and visit the sandwich shop. I eventually retired to the pub next door. Over egg and chips and successive pints of Guinness I learnt the subtext to that list. I was warned that I was in for a ride. It wasn't bad in terms of induction; indeed I was more than happy to be going home after my first day slightly pissed and having been paid double.

After a year and a half, my feelings were beginning to change about my job. If this wasn't the case then why did I feel so spectacularly free as G and I sat in our punt? The most important thing of all on that day was that I was in a boat and not in a chair. In front of me was water, above me was sky, and all around the sounds of a natural world filtered through. We stared at our floats and they stared back at us. They'd lain undisturbed and our baits had remained untroubled for several hours. We rowed the boat over to the other side of the lake which was now shrouded in damp, cool shade and we staggered around on sea legs. We debated whether to row back to the boathouse and splash out on a fry-up but that seemed to go against the spirit of the day. We had cut ourselves off from the normal comforts of life and for the sake of a meal we weren't going to check ourselves back in any earlier than we needed to.

Rowing back out, conversation picked itself up to its previous level. Optimism was renewed as our circulation began to wake our minds back up. But still very little was said. The dialogue of the natural world, as opposed to the workplace, was beginning to evolve. Here, sitting in silence didn't mean you weren't paying attention or were studiously ignoring somebody. It meant you were falling deeper into the trance of the complete and total concentration required to catch a fish. G has this theory that you never catch anything within the first two hours of arriving. Fresh from a motorway journey with the hum of modern life ringing in your ears, you spook fish with each cast, rush each strike, and generally fall into a mood of frustration and anger. Shortly after this, though, comes the feeling of nothing. You are motionless, your pulse slows, your blood thins, your speech peters out. It is then that you are on the brink of catching, because it is then that you are approaching the sense of harmony that your surroundings require before they will allow you to blend in. You normally achieve this state just at the moment when you are contemplating a 'blank'. A blank is a day spent fishing without catching a fish. It seems such an inappropriate word but it's spot on. In this state you have been wiped clean of everything you carried down to the water. You are suspended in a transcendental state. When people walk past anglers and say, 'They must be so bored,' they don't realise that the figures before them, shivering in their old hats and boots, are as holy in feeling as a yogi on Oxford Street.

And what changes a day from a blank to a result is when you absolutely and categorically *catch*. Be it the smallest of fish – even unintended quarry (more often than not it is) – to put one on the bank changes the day. It takes the yogi from Oxford Street and catapults him far, far away into the Tibetan Hills, where he lands amid mists, ancient temples and distant chanting. The opposite of a blank is total euphoria. It is not the only justification for going fishing but at the time it seems like it. Once you've landed your chosen prey from a swim that seemed a dead or an inaccessible stretch of river you are almost ready to pack it in forever. The emotion is so complete that there is a part of your brain saying, 'Don't go back! Get out whilst you can, you like room temperature and the remote control, urban life is everything, it is civilisation.' But just then a voice will break the silence, it might be yours or it might be that of your fishing companion and it will say, 'So what are you doing in a couple of weeks' time, then? I've got a Wednesday afternoon free.'

And that is how it started again. Well, not completely. G and I did blank on that first trip and ended up rowing back to the boathouse frozen and silent. But somehow that didn't matter. What mattered was that I had crossed the line, driven out of the city and gone fishing. The surroundings had restored my senses, the rhythm of the day had rebalanced my mercury. I was ready to fish on for pike and for zander and for whatever else I could find.

Chapter Four

Deborah and I lived in a '30s tenement block. As I unlocked the main door to the entrance and walked down the carpeted hallway to the lift, I felt as if I was returning from the moon. Everything was slightly out of kilter and I felt strangely distant. The doors to the lift opened with a judder that seemed suddenly severe and exact. They made me jump. I had been etherealised and was now out of step with the everyday.

The next morning I woke with the feeling that I always seem to get the day after I have been fishing. My mind always feels completely rinsed and clear but my body is shattered, as if it has been fried on re-entry to the earth's orbit. In this post-shamanic state I sat at the kitchen table and toiled slowly over my breakfast. I have never been a person to rush the morning, but that day I couldn't have even if I'd wanted to.

As going to Old Bury Hill had been G's idea I was now bound through a gentleman's agreement to return the favour and treat him to a day's fishing of my own choosing. Luckily, I had three months before the start of the next season to sort this out. I could afford to take my time over the plans, get them just right. But as spring started to turn into early summer, the smell of the air began to incite a sense of nervous anticipation within me. Rather than being able to concentrate on work, or even on reading the paper, which would normally absorb me completely, my mind drifted off to another place, to the home of the true coarse angler.

I pictured a small glassy lake, about a couple of acres, completely enclosed by mature oak woods. Above a small stream at one end stood a bleached wooden boating hut and landing stage. The stage was in disrepair, fairly rickety, with lichen growing in between the boards. A window, whose glass had cracked and was mottled by layers of mildew, blinked darkly. The roof to the boathouse had caved in and the structure lay open to the elements. Looking down the pond from here, mist rose off the water and the smell of warm earth and wild garlic was profuse. At the opposite end of the lake a small dam had been built from Victorian red brick. It had grown mossy and the brickwork had become smooth after years of rain. Between its walls water rushed down a small sluice, covered by a rusty iron grille, into a stream that ran across the floor of the woods below towards a pond. The stone at the bottom of the sluice had veins that glinted in the water. The water's edge was crowned by sets of green reeds standing like sentries and also marking the change between shallow and deep water. Here and there were sets of intense white bubbles, pricking the surface, where small insects, moths, dragonflies and water boatmen danced. Coots called and wood pigeons could be heard in the trees. The magical green pond was simmering with life. It was 3.30 a.m., dawn, on 16 June. The year could have been any one between 1880 and the present. The scene had not changed, not for decades. It had lain undisturbed by two world wars, the passing of generations, the invention of the motor car and the spread of mankind. The stolen pool, a place of impossible, Arthurian beauty.

It was the eternal estate lake, seat of the tench. Not many places like this really exist and if they do it is unlikely they are fished. They are probably tucked away on the edge of some vast country estate where the owners only fish for game as part of a social calendar. The lake would have become ornamental, a place used solely for reflection, or for children long grown up and now absent to play upon in their boats. This, or a place just like it was, I was certain, the place where I had to take G on the opening week of the next season. It would be such an antidote to the cold of Bury Hill. But here I was, no more than a mile from Victoria Station, and my nearest water was the muddy Thames which flowed by the end of our road. How was I meant to find this perfect water? The thought troubled me for days – but maybe troubled is the wrong word. No sooner had I started to think about where such a place might exist than I was transported there, flicking my bright-red float out into the water and settling back into the dawn. My reverie would then be broken by the announcer on the tube, or the click of the kettle as it boiled.

The new season arrived and the days on the calendar began to race. Still I hadn't managed to find the right water. In the flat I had an old tin trunk which had belonged to my grandfather. It had his name painted on the side, T.E. Andrews. Ours was a small flat and I had arrived as a refugee

from north London so I'd brought hardly any possessions. As
a result the trunk was crammed with objects, small items,
some of significance and some not. It was while I was
searching through this one day that I came across the answer
to my quest. It was a small circular case with gold lettering
embossed in an old Roman numeral typeface on one side
which read,

THE CREEL OF ALDERSHOT

36 STATION ROAD

TEL. 20871

It was the five-digit phone number which did it. Five
digits in a phone number seemed to hark back to a bakelite
age when the eternal pool did exist and could be fished quite
easily. The Creel, of course, was the old fishing shop in
Aldershot. Why hadn't I thought of this before? I rang
directory enquiries from the office and asked for the
Aldershot code from London. After scribbling the area code
down, which was as long as the number itself, I dialled and
waited.

A voice from another lifetime answered. It was familiar, as
if in a dream, but so obviously real. I became uneasy in my
chair, my stomach turned and my skin chilled. I asked if the
Farnham Angling Society was still in existence and, if so,
whether it was possible to join. 'Hold on,' went the voice at
the other end. I heard footsteps walking slowly away from
the phone. Moments later I heard them returning and then
the voice in the receiver. 'I've still got your details, we keep
them for fifteen years whenever a membership lapses. You're
just in time.'

I couldn't believe it. Where else would a club keep you on

file for as long as fifteen years on the off-chance that you might return? The voice continued, 'You're lucky. Another year and you'd have had to have paid an additional five pounds to join for this season.' I replaced the receiver. On a piece of paper in front of me I had the address of The Creel, the details of the amount I needed to send to renew my membership and to obtain an assorted box of start-up tackle. I looked up and around at the faces of the people in the office. Most were on the phone, shut away in their own little worlds, tied to their tasks, in trances of daily habit. I too was beginning to feel as if I was in a different place, but one that had little to do with either task or habit.

For days later, I got up early and waited for the postman. The figures on the willow pattern on my coffee cup took on a new meaning. Bleary-eyed, I played Mr Wolf with them, expecting them to come to life and start dancing in front of my eyes. The postman would have with him the parcel sent from The Creel. One morning just as I was giving up hope, he came along our landing and instead of flicking open the letterbox he rang the doorbell. I opened the door and there he stood, with a brown cardboard parcel in his hands, silhouetted by the fierce July sunshine. And for a moment I could have sworn that he wasn't dressed in a regulation Royal Mail sky-blue shirt, with a red shoulder bag slung over his shoulder, but an old reversible towelling jacket, Army and Navy chinos and desert boots.

I closed the door and sat down at the table. Using the old kitchen scissors I started to cut the brown parcel tape. Inside the box was a collection of green-stalked, red-and-yellow-topped floats for tench fishing; some line wound round a plastic spool with a Michelinesque French illustration on the side; a dispenser of Thames shot; a packet of hooks; and a plummet. The plummet was just the right shape and size to be a diving bell for the willow people on my cup. You used it for checking the depth. In the hands of an expert it could be deadly. In an envelope was a handwritten receipt and my permit. The paper had been stamped with an old block stamp and the blue ink had faded and smudged at the top of the page. The cheque that I'd sent was five pounds or so over but a hand had knowingly written, 'I'll keep the balance over for the next time.'

The permit wasn't what I had expected at all. Instead of just the primitive card I had envisaged there was a handbook, complete with black-and-white stills of most of the waters. Each water was sketched out and a description of the fishing that could be found there lay opposite it. There were road directions and rotas for night fishing. There were a lot more waters than I remembered there ever being. For some reason I didn't feel comfortable with this new version; it was too organised and defined. What I expected I don't know – perhaps for the box to fall open and all of the old tackle I'd once owned to have fallen out in starbursts onto the table.

I rang G that day and we booked in our date to go the following week. As it was the summer, the sun rose a lot earlier and a very early start was necessary. I told G just to turn up, bring a light rod and I would supply the rest. I'd bought him a guest ticket which I'd arranged to be sent to him in the meantime. In a decadent moment I had bought an old Garcia Mitchell 300 of my own, from Ben Maurice-Jones's stall at Portobello Market. Its black paint was peeling and the clutch was a bit sticky but to me it felt like a classic. I was going to pair it up with my first-ever proper fishing rod, the eleven foot Olympic tubular fibreglass Model H-1103L. This was what I had used to conjure gudgeon and roach in my first years of fishing. It had been a Christmas present from my parents that first season. All I had to do was dust it down from the back of a cupboard.

Come the morning, we swaggered down the A316 and onto the M3, heading west into the gleam, the decades stripping back every ten miles or so. There was one stretch as we got past Junction 3 where all we could see were gorse bushes in flower and ancient pine forests brooding in the distance. This is the gateway from the town to the country. Here you can sense the ghosts of old Surrey Heath swooping under a dramatic sky, their cries echoing forever across the surrounding landscape. G had no stereo in his car at this time but if he had I am certain we'd have been arguing over whether we should be listening to Vaughan Williams or The Clash, Verdi or LKJ. It was that kind of a morning, redolent of a pastoral era and riding on a fugitive spirit as London shrank behind us in the mirror.

We were going to Stockbridge Pond. The water lay at the end of an old farm track and to get to it we had to drive through stunning countryside. There were narrow lanes cut out of tall banks, boxed by hedges with sweeping cornfields rising up gently to meet the horizon. Just before we reached Stockbridge we crossed the River Wey on a bridge that was a combination of old flint and wooden girders. A white pub squatted to the left and overlooked a triangular, sloping cricket pitch. The whole scene seemed comprised of marzipan, it was so idyllic and hallucinatory. It didn't seem real. The yellow brick road had to start somewhere nearby.

Instead, we turned left at the top of the green and drove down through the sandy pot-holes to an iron gate. One of the items which had arrived in the post along with my permit was a key. It is a normal Yale type but it is as if it has Narnianesque powers. When I am feeling trapped in the city I can get my keys out and turn this one over and over in my hands. It takes me to that padlock on the iron gate, which once unlocked allows me to sweep into a grassy car park hidden by sets of trees. The dawn was well and truly up by the time the engine cut and we peeled our sticky backs from the car seats. Through the leaves the sun shone off the water and the distant click of a bail arm could be heard bouncing off the pond. We left the tackle in the car and went for a walk.

The pond matched the vision. Silver birch, small oaks and nettle beds overhung it all the way round except where swims had been cut out in the sand. Every now and again one of these would be occupied by a still figure crouched over a rod, watching a float in the margins. At the opposite end of the lake, a small dam had been built from Victorian red brick. On it was a small plaque to the man responsible for building this tribute to Capability Brown. It explains that a man called Alan Peach died in 1974 before the work he put in on the water could be realised. I remember reading it with my father and thinking that 1974 was only yesterday. Now it was history, along with long-wave radio, *Sport on 2* and *The Fishing Race*. (*The Fishing Race* had been a bizarre television programme about celebrities and anglers [whose status reversed during the programme] who travelled across Europe in old caravans, trying to clock-up catches in a given time. A Clive James-type narrator gave a sarcastic commentary in what was an unwitting precursor to *The Hitch Hiker's Guide to the Galaxy*.)

One evening back then, when we'd come out to look at the water, Dad had got chatting to an angler on the far bank. Despite the conversation the angler's eyes stared straight ahead and his mouth remained clamped round his cigarette. He was watching his float, about twenty feet out in between the beds of weed which seemed to choke the pool. It was only fishable in one or two gaps in the weed. Within minutes his float vanished and he hooked and landed a tench of about two and a half pounds. It was different from any fish I'd seen before. It had tiny scales and was an intense, dark bottle-green colour. It had thick orange lips, almost tropical in appearance. Its fins were bold, its tail like a spade. These fish don't come willingly to the bank, they hug the bottom of the lake, their muscular shoulders and bullet-like heads thudding the rod top round. This was the biggest fish I had ever seen and certainly the first-ever tench I'd seen. The angler asked if I wanted to put it into his keep net. But the fish slipped out of my grasp and escaped the net before swimming off. The angler laughed at my awe, as if catching one was simple. On many occasions we went back and tried to emulate him, but to no avail – those invisible occupants of the lake had shrunk away, captors of my imagination.

Now, though, there were no knowing anglers, just a collection of grim pensioners, their pushbikes propped up against the trees, indulging in a chain letter of a conversation. It appeared to start at one end of the bank and carry its way down to the other, stopping at each swim to be enlightened by another gem. On telling them that we'd driven down from London the conversation stopped as they eyed us suspiciously. One of them had probably been to London once, had obviously not liked what he had seen and come back sharpish. They were of the age that they neither cared nor wished to make new acquaintances.

I'd chosen Stockbridge Pond because it was physically and spiritually the closest the Farnham Angling Society could offer to match the perfect water. Also, the fish it contained were some of the most talismanic you could find – the aforementioned tench or 'doctor' fish, the crucian carp and the rudd. For years they lived in one dimension on colour plates in *The Observer Book of Fish*. They were like Darwinian exhibits. I was left to imagine what they looked like in the flesh. I had actually caught a couple of tench, but only when fishing for carp and that didn't count. The crucian carp were small cousins of the larger king or wild carp which populated only a few waters in England. The rudd was like an Irish version of the roach, more poetic and elusive and only to be found in the quietest of backwaters. In addition to this, the water also held a head of perch, those spined and striped predators who lived in deep holes or hid in the reeds, and a few out-of-season trout who normally fell to a coarse bait within weeks of the season beginning. They were popular species to fish for but they had a kudos as well. They all represented a more somnolent side to fishing. If we could catch the uncatchable, then surely we would be on the verge of fishing in the unfishable and being taken off to a world unknown. The omens seemed right. The pensioners had been catching tench, rudd and crucians all morning.

At the top end of the pond there were a couple of swims tucked away out of the earshot and eyeline of the home guard. The water was generally believed to be a bit shallower there, as the pond silted up towards a marsh, overgrown with alder. We decided we would fish there. In addition to the fibreglass match rod, I had brought with me the old split-cane fly rod which my father had used to coax roach out of Lodge Pond. It, too, had lived a charmed life and been consigned to the back of the cupboard rather than sacrificed to the small ads when I'd left home. It was a poignant moment; I was returning to a water we had both fished, albeit unsuccessfully. Tackling it up with a Garcia Mitchell, a three pound breaking-strain line, a float, some shot and a size fourteen hook was not easy. Did I understand what I was letting myself in for? A mixture of emotions crowded in on me. On the one hand I had a sense of sheer and utter pleasure, innocent almost, in that I was reviving this physical link with the past; on the other, the horror of the subsequent memories it inevitably evoked. If it was possible to feel sick and contented at the same time then I did so. G was sitting only six feet away from me but he seemed blurred, as if rendered still by a passing Impressionist painter, cut off in a limbo. It was as if I had lost the ability to hear or see. My senses broke up like a distant radio signal, lost on a dial, fading in and out. I clicked the bail arm back and cast.

The float cocked in the water and I put the rod down on its rests. After a few more casts nothing was happening. The rod was so old and brittle that I couldn't reach more than a few feet with it. This would have been fine if we had been round the other side but here the water by the bank was really shallow. I was debating whether to change rods when my mind was made up for me. On attempting a cast, the line got caught in the rod tip and I heard a splitting noise. A slight crack appeared at the top of the rod. All those fallow years had taken their toll. The rod was unusable. The magic wand was broken.

It was not meant to be like this, the return to the idyll – awkward, full of snags and haunted with unease. I finally tackled up the Olympic and was back fishing. The float sat a good fifteen feet out beyond the dipping branches of an oak and to the right of a set of lily pads. G had already been fishing for a bit as I was going through my fiasco of nostalgia. No such ghosts for him. Today was unloaded, insignificant in terms of emotional baggage. The sun had risen fully and even at 10 a.m. you could feel that the day was going to be savagely hot. A few lazy bites came and went but in fifteen years I had forgotten how to strike correctly and, rusty, I missed them. G was drifting his float and bait round the corner of the reeds to the right of the swim and soon landed a couple of golden crucians. This was reason for celebration in itself. Back in 1979 the crucian was as rare to me as a coelacanth, almost a figment of the imagination. Here, they seemed to be thriving once again, fighting like Chinese firecrackers, real oriental impostors.

As the day progressed I became slowly hypnotised by the combination of the hot sun and my float. Neither seemed to move but both possessed me. On the other side of the pond, the bank and a strip of water, as far as fifteen feet out, lay in shade. Muttering to G, I gathered my tackle and wandered off round to the other side. Once out of the sun my mind seemed to wake up. I felt certain that I would catch something here. Baiting up with breadflake, one of the quintessential 'between-the-wars' baits, I cast out. The float lay at forty-five degrees in the ripple. Within a second it had gone, snatched from the surface with a severity that made me start. It came back before I could even think of striking. Cursing, I reeled in, baited up again and recast. This time I made no mistake and the rod top slammed round. This was no crucian. Or at least I thought so, but who was I to know? The fish scudded along the bottom, thwacking the top section of the rod round and making the clutch squeal and click. Minutes later a deep-green tench lay still at my feet, in the water. I unhooked him. He must have weighed about a pound, maybe even a pound and a half. But the weight did not matter. I smiled and could feel myself welling up. In the fifteen absent years my fishing instincts hadn't slowly sharpened. But I'd had a sudden urge to walk round and try this side. It was just an idea, wasn't it? Or was it the work of some guardian angel, sitting somewhere beyond the trees, watching the whole scene in a mixture of approval and amusement, prompting me to get up from my slumber and try somewhere new? If this symbolism could be expressed how better to do it than by catching the tench? After all, this was the elusive 'doctor' fish, fêted as far back as medieval times for having medicinal properties. Perhaps I hadn't needed it when we had fished for it back then. Perhaps that was why that angler had laughed so long ago. Perhaps he knew that there would be a time when the need to catch one would be far greater than the wish.

Minutes later I caught another one. A brace of tench before lunch. It was as Walton had intended. I walked back round to where G was fishing and suggested that we break for lunch. Driving back up the track, I felt as if I had been in the open air for a lot longer than a morning. We drove on past the village green and across country, down a lane with sharply cut banks of hedge on each side, and came out opposite an old hotel. Inside, the bar smelt of winter, a mixture of stale beer and furniture polish. Any other time that would have been more than enough of a welcome. But on this day we were followers of the sun, so we toasted our success outside. The clock stopped around three. Birds sang. Song upon song. The heady potion of midsummer lay mustily across the surrounding fields. Sunshine glinted off the nearby River Wey. I knew that the best fishing lay before us. Everything was perfect. We had already caught the fish we'd come for and now the lager lulled our minds and the conversation became soporific.

The bell for last orders awoke us and we headed back to Stockbridge. I felt as if I been woken up from a long sleep. I needed tea. We brewed up at the bank side and promptly started to catch. The water was now completely in shade and the summer's evening was beginning to stretch. It was G's turn for tench and he was hauling them out. The crucians competed with them for the net. It was non-stop fishing, a bite a cast, a fish every other. We stayed on until ten. As dusk approached, the larches on the opposite bank took on a Norwegian blue tint. Instead of smelling the air you could taste it, the richness trapping in the back of your throat. A humidity rose off the water and weighed the overhanging branches down further towards it. Light values changed every second; the blues, greens and browns slipping slowly through a kaleidoscopic time lapse. Again, the fish had become a sideshow. Yes, it was a pond on the borders of Hampshire but for moments it became a bewitched place in the land of the midnight sun. I did not want to leave. Any sense of sadness and mourning had evaporated, squeezed out of my system by the slow passage of the hours. We packed our gear up reluctantly and walked back round to the car. At the dam end we stopped and looked back down the pool. A moon, almost full, had risen and cast itself across the water. Up on the trunk of an oak tree was a wooden, hand-painted sign. In shaky italics, the words FARNHAM ANGLING SOCIETY – PRIVATE FISHING – PERMITS ONLY could be made out in the half-light. I tapped my breast pocket and I was sure I could feel the imaginary outline of an old yellow card. I smiled inwardly and said thank you.

We drove out of the lane that led away from the pond. The sky in the west was blood red, like an Anglo-Saxon portent. We stopped at the Barley Mow pub, to clean up and reconnect with the world before the drive back to London. We sat with our drinks at a table outside. The moon had risen more fully and we could make out the letters on our beer mats quite easily. Although we had spent the day fishing together, we had done so separately in many ways. It was just like *The Deer Hunter*. You drink too much in the pub the night before you go and joust over who will catch what. On arriving you may fight over tackle or sides of swims, neither wanting to up the ante too much. And gradually you withdraw and disengage, as you tune into the rhythm of what's around you.

For All Those Left Behind

At the end, when you drive back into town, the boot loaded down with stinking gear, a more normal conversation returns and you laugh and joke and take the piss. Whatever it was, G and I knew to obey the rule of space and silence, the male pact. Switch off; no time for idle gossip, just serious contemplation. It was no coincidence that monks had been into their fishing in the Middle Ages. Maybe that was the ultimate brotherhood of the angle. Sure, there were anglers just like that, but we weren't in danger of losing touch with everything else. There were a good sixty people in the pub that night. Fifty-eight inside the smoky saloon, happy in the cosy confines of pub chat and two others outside, backs against the wall, talking intermittently about where they would fish next and when.

Chapter Five

We would not fish again for a long time, however. G and I both moved house and lost touch with each other as well as ourselves. Even the healing powers of that trip to Stockbridge and its bidding had not been enough to prise us away from the demands of our daily lives. A line was not wet again for the rest of that season. Perhaps that summer's day had been so perfect that there was a need to preserve it and try not to repeat it. Perhaps there were other reasons, too.

Come the next close season, however, things were beginning to straighten themselves out somewhat and this time we both applied to The Creel for permits. By now I had no qualms about calling the old place up. What had before felt like an act of subversion now felt as natural as anything. Was there a complacency about to set in with my fishing? Was I ready to accept that it was going to be a regular thing in my life again? Those first two trips had become iconic almost, marking the end and the beginning of a season. Had I thought that it would be that simple? Just paying the respects twice a year and expecting that to be enough? I think at the start I had thought that. Despite their wonder and to some extent their natural glory, both occasions had disturbed me a great deal. It is one thing to remember someone who had died in an abstract way, by recalling a memory, or by looking at a photograph. It is another thing, completely, to do what I had done. It was like turning the clock back, like stepping into a time machine, one whose mechanics had warped with age so that everything was not as it was before. The trees were taller, the water easier. I had been haunted by those two days; the first one because I really did feel as if I was regressing, and the second one because of its magic realism. Both stayed with me for a very long time, drifting in and out of my daydreams and bewitching me. I am sure that that was one of the real reasons why I didn't go again for over a year. I was still absorbing every sound, every sight and smell, still trying to come to terms with what it all meant.

I shied away from confronting it completely by avoiding the issue. It was easier to work than to fish. I did not have the energy or the impulse to go back so soon. I think, also, that I was not strong enough to turn around and look at the facts coldly. Going to a place where my father and I shared our best moments had been in some manner a way of keeping him alive. I had strong feelings that he had been my guardian angel that first day at Stockbridge. In the year that followed that, however, the slow and agonising reality began to hit home. It had taken nearly five years, but I think I was beginning to accept that my father was gone. And that he was never going to come back.

In the hour immediately after he died, I sat with him for a while, both of us alone, and I watched the second hand tick round on his watch. The undertaker wasn't due until later in the afternoon and I felt it rude to leave Dad by himself whilst we were in the house. A vigil of sorts. And I had kept that vigil well beyond that afternoon, for months and years afterwards, sitting in my own worlds, in pubs and crowds, alone and in company. A little part of me always hoping, always waiting. Waiting for him to wake up, wink at me and say, 'Alright, son?'

And after that day at Stockbridge he winked at me a lot – in the faces of people on the tube and walking down the street; in the faces of people in newspaper photographs and advertisements. He started to come back to life a lot more. But just as he did so, he would drift away again without saying anything, his features getting fainter and his expression more confused. I had to face reality. But to do so I had to go to places which nurtured a terror within me. The riverbank or lakeside lacked the distractions of the city. In London months could go by without you even having to stop and think about anything in particular. Everything was caught up in a maelstrom of routine. Work, home, supper, TV, bed, work, pub, gig, club, work, bed, weekend, sleep. Once you got past Christmas there was no stopping you until the next one. Each year seemed shorter, each month passed before you'd got used to the change it brought. I think I was running away and was just seeking to fill every hour and the ones ahead so that I would never have to ask myself the questions – where is he and why isn't he coming back?

So, when G ordered a permit along with mine I was relieved. Relieved that I wasn't going to have to face that all by myself. Fishing alone and confronting the past alone were too much to consider at that time. Of course, at the time I didn't realise that this was the case. Having a fishing partner was as good a way as any of avoiding the issue of why I was going and for what. Our trips were always loaded with sharp humour and bonhomie, and it was good just to get out of London. We both agreed that a return to Stockbridge was the first thing we should consider for that coming season.

This time, we didn't have to leave it until July; this time we could go in the magical first week of the season. We booked a day out and once again ventured off down the M3. It was a day as similar to the last as you could imagine. It was a month earlier in the year, though, so the countryside was fuller and thick with bloom. By lunchtime we had taken another splendid bag of tench, crucians and even some rudd. The fishing was so easy. If there were any horrors there they had yet to materialise. The morning was fresh and hot. It turned my mind away from anything other than the next five minutes. The weather was such that it was easy to believe in the saying, 'Tomorrow is another day.' We headed for the pub at around one to enjoy a very slow pint and some lunch. As we sat at the bench, we flicked through the new permits and began to discuss the other waters that Farnham leased.

G was agitated. He felt it was all too tame, too rural and comfortable. Of course, he was taking it at face value so I shouldn't have been surprised that he felt like that. I didn't want to go somewhere else, my real business was unfinished. But in all my obsession with Stockbridge Pond I had almost forgotten that there were other waters available for us both to fish now that G was a member of FAS. After a muted discussion, a battle of wills ensued, which was resolved by the offer of another drink, and soon we were looking at where

else we could go in the afternoon. In the weeks before I'd had
a phone conversation with one of the bailiffs who looked after
a water close to Stockbridge, the River Wey. He'd given me a
few tips as to how to fish it so I suggested that we gave that
a go. G was well into this – a river, proper fishing, nothing
ornamental or artificial. I had fished Farnham's stretch of the
Wey once only. It had been with Dad, inevitably, one winter's
afternoon. And now, one summer's afternoon, my courage
'Dutched' by a pint, I knew I was ready. Ready to find his
ghost, not to alter my gaze and embrace it.

We left the pub and took the road to Elstead, across
another wooden bridge at the opposite corner of the green.
The cornfields baked all around us and it was very easy to
believe that we were part of an island community, self-
sufficient through the riches of the land. I gazed out of the
window of the car thinking of John Schlesinger's screen
version of *Far from the Madding Crowd*. It was my favourite
film. On a day such as this it could be none other. If the
journey on the motorway stripped time back by a decade a
mile, this one going from one small country village to
another seemed to strip back the centuries. I half expected to
see Terence Stamp wandering across the horizon, arm in arm
with Julie Christie.

To get to the Broomfield Cottage stretch of the Wey, we
drove along a narrow lane lined with rhododendrons and
turned right down a rutted, sandy track. We pulled up in a
small clearing next to some woods which eventually led to
the river. Here, the cornfields were broken up by huge oak
trees, many hundreds of years old, which stood like
prehistoric scarecrows in the summer heat. Occasionally, odd

branches would stick out, like desperate fingers, devoid of leaves, gnarled and spiky, made lame by an ancient thunder storm. The drone of bees was the only sound other than the occasional distant tap of a woodpecker. After the order of Stockbridge Pond and its environs we were now in a wilder country.

We were going chub fishing. To do this we just needed to tackle up one rod each at the car, take a bottle of water, a landing net and some bait, and set off through the wood and fields to find the river. It was great to be going fishing unencumbered by bags, chairs and holdalls. It was the kind of day when you can walk forever, daring the dusk never to fall. Inside the wood the air was cooler and every sound was muffled by the canopy of leaves. The earth was mossy and bouncy. Wild bracken grew like a carpet across the floor. After a few hundred yards we stepped over a stile and another vista spread out before us – miles and miles of fields stretching away to a heat haze, some of corn, some of grass, again broken only by the odd oak and, running through the middle of it all, a river. Cows watched lazily as we crossed the fields towards it. On reaching it, the banks were steep and completely overgrown by a mass of nettle and hawthorn. A barbed-wire fence had been erected presumably to keep the cattle from reaching for an extra meal and ending up in the drink. There was little space to fish. It was a toss-up between resting on the wire or immersing yourself in the nettles. The river, from the near bank to far, was about fifteen to twenty feet at its widest, and a morass of streamer weed broke the surface frequently, mixed in with floating buttercups. Dragonflies patrolled up and down. Although it had been hot, we'd had a fair bit of rain recently and the river was quite full, the colour of golden pale ale. It was a classic southern chalk stream that fed the farmland around us.

G and I split up and headed off in separate directions. Here and there, a tree, growing out into the river and covering it in shade, would offer some shelter. Barbed-wire fences were not sufficient to break their falls, and once or twice there was a stretch which housed a half-submerged set of branches, broken off in winter storms and spate. If I looked out of place in the landscape, I didn't feel it. For once I could say I was English and it felt like an instinctive claim. A shout from the belly. The river snaked its way in a succession of slow U-turns through the fields for about a mile and a half. I fished each swim for about fifteen minutes, just as I'd been instructed. That was as long as it was meant to take to find a feeding chub, a shy but greedy fish which would materialise silently from underneath the roots of a tree or an overhanging bank, open its pillar-box mouth and gorge your bait. I was using hunks of luncheon meat which I had dyed red to make them more visible in the water. After a couple of hours I felt faintly absurd. There I was wandering the banks, biteless, fishless, with luminous hands, pouring with sweat, having been bitten by what felt like a thousand mosquitoes. Moreover, I hadn't seen a fish all afternoon. The river just flowed by, slowly hypnotising me with its swathes of weed rolling back and forth in the broken current. Then, just as I was in fear of the spell breaking, I caught a chub. The rod tip tapped twice and was then pulled right round. I hooked it with a lazy strike. The line cut into the weed and the river soon gave the fish up like a pearl from an oyster. It was the first chub I had ever caught. As with most significant catches it weighed no more than a pound and a half.

As the afternoon wore on I wandered back up to find G. The landscape was torpid, yawning, and I was sunburnt. I could feel it on the backs of my ears and on my neck. My eyes ached from the glare of the water and every joint felt sore. But the evening was approaching and with it the promise of cool air and more fish. G hadn't had anything but was encouraged by my catch. We shared a cup of tea and parted once again like opposing chess pieces being moved from one end of the board to the other.

In his wisdom the bailiff had told me about a swim which had been on my mind all day. It was in the corner of one of the fields. I stepped over the barbed wire and into the lee of the river's bend. A bed of sand, washed up by flood water, led down to the water's edge and nettles grew, six, seven, eight feet, in hordes all around. The field had a corner here because the river changed course and bent round, almost at forty-five degrees. A tree obscured the bend completely, but it was possible to stand and cast into the flow in front of it and let my bait be carried around the corner. The bed of the river deepened there and chub were said to lie up in the hole. I baited up and cast, the rig landing with a satisfying splash before resting about ten feet round the corner, out of sight. A couple of minutes later, the rod tapped and then shot into a curve and I was into a much larger chub. Its shyness forgotten, it careered around the corner and set off angrily upstream. I applied some side strain and halted it, whereupon it seemed to become disorientated, unused to its new surroundings. I whistled for G to bring the landing net;

he'd seemed convinced that if anyone was going to need it, it would be him. Either he couldn't hear me or was ignoring me (probably the latter), as he didn't show. I played the fish against the current for another five minutes before I was sure it was spent and then beached it amongst the nettles. Its diamond-shaped bronze scales seemed iridescent in the dusk.

It was a wild fish. There was a good chance that it had never been caught before. I photographed it for posterity, held it in the shallows and watched as it shimmered back into its hole, the epitome of stealth, a shadow with fins.

G turned up a moment later, out of breath, having run the length of the stretch to see what the fuss was about. He'd had no luck and was ready to pack up. I was too, but although I'd had a couple of fish, the majesty of the countryside that afternoon was what stayed with me as we picked our way towards the now dark woods which sat at the foot of the azure sky. House lights from the farm cottage glowed away to our right and underfoot a dew was settling on the grass. The car was sitting obediently in the half light as we stumbled out through the branches. As we drove off down the path towards the road, rabbits leapt from the headlights into the bracken. In the beam of the light I was still looking for my expected ghost to step out in front of us, yards ahead, but it never appeared. G sat silently in the car next to me as we drove towards the nearest pub and I can't be certain, but I think I was whistling. I was definitely cheerful.

But I knew that it wouldn't be as easy as that. Fishing that day was like opening up a razor wound. You don't feel the cut initially. It makes you start, but it is not until later that it causes pain and discomfort. There is always the possibility that the sun had made me a touch delirious as well. I should have known better. In the weeks that followed, and even now, that day on the river became a nightmare which returns to me. Always, it is fused with the real trip I had taken with my father years before. On one side of the river, the side upon which I am standing, the countryside is bathed in that glorious summer splendour. But I am not fishing. I have put my rod and my bag down and am wandering, anxiously, up and down the bank. Clambering through the nettles, catching clothes and skin on barbed wire, searching. My eyes are scanning the opposite bank. The landscape there is different. It is midwinter. The trees are bare. The nettle banks have died and wind whistles through the barbed-wire fences, creating a low whine. The fields are dark brown and the sky is the colour of lead. I am looking for my father, but he is nowhere to be seen. All the time I am running, towards the bend in the river where we once fished together, frantic in the belief that he will be there, that all will be well once again. When I reach it, though, there is a catch. The side we fished is now the summer side. And I know that he is on the winter one.

This was all becoming too much for me. I was not one for being haunted – it felt ridiculous but when you wake at 5.30 a.m. and you have been crying in your sleep there is not a lot that you can do about it. What was worse was that now I actually wanted to go fishing more than anything. And I couldn't work out if it was because I wanted to carry on searching and exorcising, or whether it was because I had caught the bug which I'd once had as a child and a teenager. Then one day the number 73 bus was rerouted on my way home from work. Instead of taking me up Albion Road, it drove me up Green Lanes, and out of the window I noticed an illuminated sign. It read 'Fishing Tackle'. The shop was Ashpoles of Islington – a famous name which I'd heard of but had presumed was in Islington itself, not Newington Green.

On the following Saturday, my curiosity got the better of me and I set off to the shop to have a nose around. It was another Creel. Mecca once more. Inside, conversations were taking place across the counter, tackle was festooned from every surface and the smell of bait filled the air. I approached the counter and asked the man behind it if I could buy some tackle. I didn't need any, but I could hardly bowl into a place I didn't know, stride up to the counter and start regaling everyone with my troubles. I needn't have worried though. As soon as I started to ask for some tackle, I was asked where I fished and for what. Ten minutes later I'd still not bought any tackle, and the owner laughed to himself and said, 'So, a fisherman reborn.' I bought a couple of classic perch floats, some line and some hooks and left. As the weeks went on and summer turned to autumn my visits to the shop became more frequent. I got to know the people there and was happy with my new mantle. It seemed to fit in so many ways. On one occasion we started to talk about where you could fish within London and it struck me that here was a perfect compromise. I could still fish and pay homage but wouldn't have to go to places which had so much personal history.

And so it was that I joined the London Anglers' Association, founded in 1884 – when the lanes would have been green and the road would have got you to Albion a lot quicker than it does now. The association has access to over forty waters, most of them rivers, all within a couple of hours' drive from most of London. I persuaded G to join and we began to plan a trip to eclipse our day at Old Bury Hill Lake. Mike, the man at the counter, had convinced me that pike fishing on rivers was much more exciting than on still water, and as rivers were what predominated in the members' handbook, a river it was. We chose the River Lea at Rye House near Hoddesdon in Hertfordshire. Neither G nor I had a clue what it was like but Mike assured us that it was a reasonable stretch. The sketch in the handbook was crude, but all the better for it, and was adorned, as all the pages were, with a compass which looked as if it had been copied from an ancient mariner's map. It had the right aesthetic, suitably nostalgic but miles from Hampshire.

The morning that G and I set out was dark and very cold. He picked me up at about 6.30 a.m. on a December day and we drove off through empty streets, up through Tottenham and out onto the M11. Inevitably, we got lost, the map being fit for a traveller on a horse and cart but it had obviously not been updated since 1884 when it had first been drawn. Sitting in a petrol station, whilst G asked for directions, the need for a hand-drawn compass made a lot of sense. Soon, though, we'd updated the old version with a biro by adding a few roundabouts and the spectre of the motorway, and driving through an old council estate eventually found ourselves on the banks of the Lea. In the days of Izaak Walton, patron saint of the angler, no doubt this was a quiet rural backwater. How it had changed. I suggested to G that we were more lost than we'd originally thought. The only thing which lit the darkness was the sulphurous glow of a light from a neighbouring concrete factory. It sat grimly on the bank about fifty yards away. We could see no sign of human life, but it didn't even seem as if any was needed. The vast towers and vats hissed and belched by themselves. The hum of a generator, or from the electric fence which encircled it, was the only thing which penetrated the eerie silence. The river was inky black, fringed with ice and looked as if it had ceased to flow. A towpath cut its way along next to it, and stretched away into the gloom, broken only by the odd strangled hawthorn bush. It was desolate and oppressive and savagely unwelcoming. 'Perfect,' said both G and I, thinking that in such an inhospitable place the pike would surely be found and that she would probably be very hungry.

We unpacked our gear from the boot of G's car, locked up, and set off down the towpath, the sharp frost biting through the soles of our boots. Closer to, the factory was even more sinister. I felt certain that it no longer produced concrete and instead processed people. I was glad to get past it. Further down the bank things became slightly more rural. Patches of wasteland appeared on either side of the bank and trees occurred at intervals. Soon, we came to a bend in the river where a deep pool opened out before turning another corner and rushing off downstream. As an angler you hope you have an instinct for where the fish might be. I felt certain that this place would be home to several. We put our gear down. The light was bright enough for us to be able to see our breath. The sky was lightening to the east, glowing like a paraffin lamp. At first it had yellowed slightly but that started to give way to a deeper blue and then a deep scarlet. G joked that we'd made it as far as the Steppes. Welcome to the Gulag.

The factory took on yet more worrying symbolism.

Setting up was a painful, slow process as my bones set in the cold and my movement dulled. It took me a good ten minutes to put a bait in the water. The orange top of my pike bung plopped into the river like a stone into treacle. Then it settled, the dawn really began to break and with my first coffee and half-frozen pie, hopes began to raise themselves. The grass at the side of the riverbank began to turn slowly from white to blue, from blue to green. A pale, apologetic sun rose above the field opposite. Nothing stirred, my float remained still. The water froze in my rod rings after each cast. It was impossibly cold, but my anticipation was equal to it. The more extreme the conditions, the more I felt I was bound to catch something. The morning progressed and as it did, so the environment became tamer and the chances and hopes of catching became slimmer in my mind. At lunchtime, my blood thick and my pulse slow, I caught up with G, who was fronting it out further downstream. He'd had nothing. In the half-light earlier, we'd noticed a large building close to where we'd parked the car. We tramped back towards it, praying that it was a pub.

Passing the factory we could see the building clearly. It was a huge old '30s pile with a pub sign hanging outside. To the left of it was a corrugated iron fence and within that were dozens of gypsy caravans, half submerged in mud and rubbish. We walked over to the pub. I was so cold that on entering the fug inside I felt sick. The smell of British cooking lay heavily throughout the bar. It was quiet, with only a few lunchtime drinkers who had retreated to the furthest corners of the place. Having ordered pies and chips we took our drinks and went and sat in one of the unoccupied corners. Our minds started to thaw and we became more aware of the atmosphere in the place. Conversations were carried on at a whisper and every so often a couple more people would come in, order their drinks and creep into the shadows. We were eyed suspiciously as our food arrived. All the other customers were on a strict diet of export lager and Superkings or JPS. We were the only people not dressed in a regulation pleated leather jacket, drip-dry trousers, towelling socks and scuffed loafers. It was hard not to overhear others' conversations as there was no music, just crashes from the kitchen. Finishing our food quickly and dispensing with the idea of another drink, we made ourselves scarce.

Once across the road and back down the towpath with our tackle, I felt as though I could breathe more easily. You could imagine that the pub wasn't one that you just dropped into uninvited. Everyone had an agenda, and for certain, ours was the only one that involved extracting things from the river rather than depositing them there. The day was getting more and more surreal. We traipsed back down to the bend and kept on going, eager to see what the rest of the stretch had to offer. Half a mile or so further on, the river split into two at the head of an island. Dotted around it were cheap river cruisers with green algae lines painted round their hulls. To our right was a concrete bridge over which artics thundered on their way to Harwich and the Hook of Holland. We fished our baits hard under the boats, at the head of the island and in front of a small reed bed which had died back on the far bank. Between the island and the bridge was a set of telegraph wires, and under these was a sign warning anglers not to fish under them for risk of electrocution. Wherever you turned there seemed to be an impending sense of doom and a chill of unease. It was hard to concentrate on the fishing. The surroundings were so insidious, they crept under your skin and made you restless. It didn't feel like a place in which you wanted to settle. The afternoon darkened and the sun set against the bridge. The air grew colder with each minute.

By dusk everything had become completely still. The edges of the bank began to lose definition as the darkness approached. I could just make out the orange of my pike bung as it slid across the surface of the river and disappeared. I struck and met a solid resistance. Then the fish shot towards me in a bid to get under the bank. I reeled in my line as quickly as I could but it was too late, in the slackness the bait had been dropped. The smelt had the characteristic slashed teeth marks from a pike across its belly. I was drained and quiet, unmoved by the action, probably approaching the initial stages of hypothermia. It was appropriate that the fish had got away, unseen. Everything was slipping away here – the empty factory, the pub, the caravan site – all of it was a desperate last staging post before you fell off the edge and disconnected with regular society. It was a brutal mile, displaced and discordant. If any one day should have made me stop there and then it should have been that one. But I was more curious than ever, because rather than wanting to run from it, I wanted to go deeper, to get further into the interior. I felt that the more I cut myself off from a sense of civilisation, the more comforted I would feel. There were no spirits here to trick me, just a sense of glorious isolation.

G was adamant. He was never going back to the River Lea. As I tried to persuade him of a return trip just before Christmas he was evasive. But in a way that suited me just fine. Shortly after Christmas, I had the opportunity to go even further afield. Deborah and I were staying in the house that her father had built in Swaffham Prior on the edge of the Fens. Ironically enough, the London Anglers' Association had rights to a stretch of the River Cam close by and I had been hankering after fishing it for some time. It was in the suitably named place of Upware, allegedly east of anywhere and west of nowhere.

I climbed out of the brass bed at around 5.30 a.m., dressed, and drove off in the direction of the river. The roads were empty. To my left the sun was trying to rise but looked as if it had given up on the idea and gone back to bed. I reached Upware fairly quickly and parked the car under a group of bushes set back from the road. I gathered my tackle and walked past the red-bricked pumping station, crossed a stile and climbed down to the river. The sun had given up, the dawn was grey and a sharp wind whipped down the channel. This was a place beyond the edge, with just a few curtained bungalows on the bank opposite as the only signs of habitation. An Alsatian on a rope barked at me and chased me as far as it could, until the rope went taut. It shrank into the distance as I walked on up to the confluence of the river.

I looked out across the water which appeared as if it was in the process of freezing, the ripples getting slower and slower all the time. I was certain I was going to connect. The landscape was primitive and the weather inhospitable. I reached into my bag to get my bait, frozen herring. To my surprise there was nothing there. I'd left it behind by mistake. On another day this would have made me curse and swear. I shivered and laughed to myself. It was as if I had been meant to forget it. I hadn't come here to fish. I knelt and looked around me. The sky shone like metal. The wind bit into my face and my head felt clear. Within it I could hear my heart beating. For once I didn't have to fear its echo. It was just me and no one else. It was a sign that there could be a new beginning.

Chapter Six

The only way I felt I could find a new beginning was to turn away from anything that had a connection with the past, to fish for something new in places unfamiliar. Then, perhaps I could shrug off the ghosts and embrace the future. Of all the fish and all the styles I had known before I had never fly fished for trout. Fly fishing was an alien concept, something that other people did. There was nothing in me that made me think I would be able to fly fish, or rather, there was nothing in my heart which made me want to. For those reasons alone it seemed perfect as a choice for a new start.

I had caught trout before, by mistake, whilst I'd been trotting a worm for perch or chub on the River Wey. They were wild brownies, their pale flanks a pageant of vivid red and blue spots, each one like the thumbprint of a monk, a seal of time and faith. As ancient and with as many echoes of the past as a medieval ruin, this was a fish that thrived in rich, weedy rivers, where the streamer choked the course and old willows lay their branches down to drink. A flash of silver, the float disappearing under the surface like a dart, and one would be on, haring this way and that, upstream and downstream. It was like washing away the gravel and sand and uncovering a chalice or sword from a Viking hoard. Rarely did I ever catch one of over a pound. I caught one of about two pounds on the last day of the season a couple of years back and it had been dying already. Slow in the water, and bearing the marks of an attack from a hungry pike, it seemed to beg for sanctuary, gills pulsating, as I held it in the current to let it go. I was reluctant to withdraw the guard of my hands, as its fins twitched. I pulled my fingers away slowly and the trout edged under the overhanging bank and out of sight, deep beneath my feet, as if retiring to another world.

That other world, a promise of a future without nostalgia and its trickery. If I followed the brown trout perhaps it would show me how to deal with the onslaught of the present, how to change and yet remain almost the same as before. To exist as if camouflaged. I felt the margins and boundaries of life had shrunk since the death of my father. I lived on a different planet. I had aged, perhaps not visibly to anyone else, but on some days I was hollowed out by loss. It wasn't an obvious grief. Reason appeared to have been stripped from the world. There was no one to carry torches anymore, no one with the ability to rationalise and sympathise, to instil a sense of calm. My father may have been a soldier for most of his life, but to me he had more in common with a priest, exuding a constant sense of paternal security; someone who would always sort you out in trouble, give good counsel, wise direction and sanctuary. With him had gone a sense of morality and compassion. Occasionally I came across others in the same place as me – often drunk, blind and weary, with their loss and their box of values, newly inherited and unfamiliar to them, a new mantle, one which they were not sure how to wear.

There were not many waters in the south of England or, for that matter, anywhere in England where you could fly fish for brown trout without being royally connected or absurdly rich. So Deborah and I packed our cases, and with spring arriving flew to Scotland. Here you could fish in the hills and the only payment you would have to make would be a long walk. We stayed the first night at the hotel belonging to an old family friend of Deborah's grandmother, a man who'd introduced Deborah's parents to one another, a delightful eccentric of the old school who serenaded his dinner guests with Wagner and followed them around with newly opened bottles of champagne, insisting that everyone drank. Deborah had just lost her father and her mother had died ten years previously, so for her, parts of the trip were as much a pilgrimage as they were a crusade for me.

The next day we left the Clifton Hotel in Nairn and drove west, to the Kyle of Lochalsh, stopping for papers and chips at a roadside pub and meeting the rising road at every turn with a new sense of freedom and hope. There used to be a ferry to Skye, and as we approached the Kyle of Lochalsh I remembered a humid August evening long ago, waiting for the boat to come and carry me over the oily waters to another holiday.

There is a poem about Skye, not the most well known, but its lines had filled my mind for days and influenced my decision to seek a new dawn in yet another place so full of memories. The poem is called 'The Cuillin', after the mountains of Skye, and was written by Sorley MacLean:

> Beyond the Lochs of the blood of the children of
> men . . .
> . . . Heroic the Cuillin is seen
> Rising on the other side of sorrow.

So, I returned to the scene of the idyll, twenty years on, determined to exorcise the spirit of the eel with the grace of the wild brown trout. Old portents would remain for as long as I shied from them and more poignantly, however hard I tried to turn away, I was pulled back by a distant sense of yearning.

We spent the next night outside Portree in an old baronial castle, its walls lined with tigers' heads and stags' antlers. Long after dinner, its owner, dressed in a kilt for the benefit of the Americans staying there, stood by the piano in the drawing room and talked of his childhood, of stalking sea trout as they came up the river in late August, and of the present, taking the boat to the mainland in autumn to teach his own daughter how to fish for salmon. He also talked of a small loch, called Cuithir, in the north of the island. His family had once run a quarry and Cuithir was the flooded site of the old mine workings, high up in the hills. The loch was seldom fished but was full of native brown trout, stocked unwittingly from rivers and tarns, the eggs washed in by the spring rains. If you drove up the eastern shore of the island, past the imposing shadow of the Old Man of Storr you would eventually reach the village of Lealt. Here there were a few cottages at the end of an unmade road. If you parked and walked up past these houses you would come to the dismantled railway that had once run down from the quarry workings and been used to take stone to the mainland.

The walk from the village along the railway seemed to go on forever. The line followed the River Lealt, but with the sleepers sunken in the peat and the river overflowing it was difficult to make out exactly where we were on the map. Occasionally the river would widen and deepen into a golden pool, and from high up on the embankment above it you could see the rings on the water where trout were rising. There was a fine mist of a drizzle, floating down from the clouds above us, that masked the mountain tops until they were no more threatening than a pale shadow on a watercolour. The rich smell of peat bog rose up from the sodden ground, and as we walked it was obvious we were now a long way from the end of the village and even further from the road. A low whine of thermal wind rushed down the mountain to meet us at every turn. It kissed our ankles and bade us to climb. Suddenly, there was complete silence. It was as if the wind had been called off. Up above us were the steep sides of a giant tarn, the rocky peak of the hill shelving away sharply and descending into the water beneath. A shallow lake lay in front of us. It had no shoreline as such, the marshy ground merely giving way to beds of reeds, stunted by late snows, and then the blue water, dark and sheer as cold slate. At one end there was an outcrop, a mixture of sand and old red brick. We'd found the workings at Loch Cuithir. The owner of the castle had told me that at the height of its industry, up to 200 men lived up here, all year round, in tents pitched in the lee of the cliff. In the stillness, the smell of pipes, the shouts of men and the constant clank of old machinery filled the place. And then there was silence again.

I spun the drum on the reel so that it whirred and with a new rhythm started to pay out the fluorescent floating line into the centre of the loch. Fly casting was a new discipline. It defied gravity, it defied logic. The fly, lighter than air, a dressing of silk and feather on a small bronze hook, tied to the faintest of lines, was flicked out twenty, thirty feet, by a movement that owed more to imagination than to motion. I was fishing an imitation dry fly, a speck on the surface of the water. After an hour I was wet to the skin with rain. I walked round to the other side of the loch to where rings were dappling the surface. A hatch of midges danced on the water, just beyond a bed of reed mace. With my rod clasped between my teeth and my arms stretched out to balance myself, I waded, knee-deep through black mud, each step bringing up a putrid stench. With difficulty I pulled myself onto a clump of tight reeds that created a raft in the middle of a bay. I switched flies, tying the new one with a tight blood knot and then lifting my arms in an attempt to get the line to sing for me. The rings faded from the surface. With each cast, the wild brown trout of Cuithir, the guardians of the quarry workers and keepers of this quiet place sank away from me, beckoning me ever further off the map.

And that was where I would have to go if I wanted to follow them. On our last morning, as we said goodbye to our host, he showed me a place down near Sligachan. Sligachan lay at the brooding feet of a mountain valley, its hillsides cut with streams that raced down into a river mouth and the open sea. An H.V. Morton, writing in the '20s, gave this description of his stay in a hotel there:

> In spite of its hot baths, it aquatints and its garage, it was spiritually a mountain hut: the only place of warmth and shelter in the abomination of desolation.

The hotel still stood, and a mile and a half or so before you reached it, under the gaze of Meall Odhar Mor, a god of a mountain, was the Loch Mor na Caiplaich.

This place was said to be an oasis in the wilderness — another set of abandoned quarry workings, hidden behind an undulating lip of gorse, and distinct from the others, with water pure enough to drink and deep, too deep to measure by man. On a warm day, chrysalises hatching in the darkness of its floors and whirling up to the surface would be followed through the layers by trout — a hunter watching the silhouette of an insect as it jigged and swam towards the distant light. Maybe here I would meet my trout again.

With each climb, another ridge emerged out of the brown snow-fired grass that scorched the hillside around me. The contours on the map were very shallow and I was worried I had lost the way — until, over another brow, I could sense the water. A small, oval crater sat drying in the sun. The water was crystal clear and underneath the surface you could see the summer grasses pushing up to form a water meadow. Dragonflies settled on a couple of sprigs that poked above the surface. This was not the right water though. I walked on. I was ready to give up. I was off the map but the water I wanted was not here. In anger and frustration I turned back, my rod trailing behind me, lowered like a defeated standard. As I descended on the route I thought I'd come up by, the ground grew very boggy. I wandered round in an arc to find a firmer path. I skirted round a narrow ridge, everything dropped away to my left and I could make out a circle of birds in the sky. I walked towards them and opening up over the marsh appeared a huge piece of water, with an island in the middle. Tiny, stunted oak trees grew in solitude and defiance on its shore, frail, like flags on a mountain top. The skeletons of summer bushes covered the small island. The water was completely sheltered, in a dip of around ten or fifteen metres, shut off from view. The sky seemed closer than the earth. There was a holy atmosphere.

Deborah joined me and we had lunch in a small bay – some oatcakes and cheese and I brewed some tea. This place needed an offering of some kind and this simple gesture seemed the only thing to do. Deborah sat sketching, marking out the edges of the loch and the mountains in the distance. I picked up my rod and leapt from the bank onto sets of large stones that made up an impromptu bridge over the shallows. Going as far as I could I pulled off some line and began to cover the water with searching casts. There was no activity on the surface so I fished a wet fly, deep, its silver-and-green body visible even fifteen feet down from my vantage point above the water. I raised and spread my arms over and over again, as if in worship, but nothing. I was sure there was a time when the brown trout rose in this loch, but it was not happening now; the sun was too high and the day too bright. You'd have to be here at dawn or dusk – a tall order, because to find the loch before sunrise or the road in the dark you would need to know the hills like the back of your hand. I stopped fishing. I experienced a feeling I'd never felt before. I had come to a place to fish but once there I'd become disarmed and bewitched, the sense of beauty too intense to disturb or alter. There were reminders of loss on the island. Some places had been difficult to return to; the jetty at Broadford, the chip shop at Portree, but up here, hundreds of feet above the sea, there was also some peace, a glimpse of the other side. It was enough to know that this was where the brown trout swam. In the long grass, out of the wind, I breathed in clear air and for a moment I lay down and closed my eyes.

The new happiness, a lightness, carried us both off the island and down the west coast of Scotland, through Arisaig and into the Morvern Hills. We drove out to Ardtornish and along the banks of Loch Aline. From there we took a small roll-on roll-off ferry to the island of Mull seeing no reason to stop, and were carried across the Sound. The only town on Mull is an unexpected riot of Mediterranean colour, pastel-fronted houses standing in a neat semi-circle on the small harbour front at Tobermory. In one of the bookshops I picked up a book called *Fishing on Mull*. On the back was a sketch of the island that marked its lochs with leaping fish and its hills with soaring eagles. It was the afternoon, the pub was closing and the ferry did not leave for the mainland until six. As much as I did not want to fish anymore, revelling in the afterglow of Skye, it seemed too good an opportunity to pass up.

We drove up and out of the village towards the Mishnish Lochs. The roof of Mull was a barren place. The deciduous trees that had crowded round the houses in the harbour could not be reached by the Gulf Stream up here, and forests of pine replaced them in long rows. The sky pressed down and although it was daylight there was a permanent sense of darkness and brooding about the place. I stood on the edge of the shore and cast my fly line across the wind. It started to rain. Deborah had retreated to the car and I could see steam from a flask filling up the windscreen. I laughed. With the rain came an awkward wind and on my third or fourth back cast the leader was caught by it. The fly line paid out through the air and I peered through the gloom for the sight of my fly landing on the water. And then I felt a stab. Like a punch in the eye. A sharp pain. I knew immediately what had happened. I kept my eye open, not wanting to blink. I reached up with my hand and touched the lid. The hook had blown back across my face and the point had gone through the lid and into the back of my eye. The momentum of the line had pulled it deep. I cut the leader and walked back up to the car.

I knocked on the window and as Deborah wound it down I walked round to the driver's side to look in the mirror. Deborah got out of the car and I stood swearing, angry at myself. Deborah fainted. She'd had fits in the past when she'd fainted, so I ran round and picked her up. She woke up and apologised. After a moment she said she was fine and stood up, but collapsed again immediately, slumping against the car, her legs folding under her. I lifted her up, slapped her gently, told her to look away and asked for the car key. The eye was numb, and I could not see clearly out of it, but my other one was fine. I drove to Tobermory on the clutch, not stopping for oncoming traffic. The pharmacy was closing and the proprietor directed me to the doctor's house. I was more worried about Deborah, who was pale and white. In the surgery they made her tea and I went in to see the doctor. The ferry left in an hour so he used some pliers to push the hook right through and cut the shank and then offered to show me the jar of eyes he kept from previous anglers who'd fished on Mull. Laughing, I left, and we drove south through Salen to the ferry. My eye was full of antibiotics and we had a long drive along Loch Aline ahead of us. Deborah could not go behind the wheel for twenty-four hours. We reached the slipway in time for the last boat. I turned off the engine and we sat in the rain. The lightness had suddenly gone, the portents crowded in again. That night, when we did get to our bed, I dreamt of spines, poison, a priest in a pulpit and blindness.

Back in London, the close season for coarse fishing was still in force and there could be no healing from the tench until 16 June. In the meantime I resolved to find the brown trout again and realign myself. There was a water up the M11, an old bomb-pit of a pond on a farm, where you could fish for trout. I persuaded G that we should go, but I myself wasn't convinced. Here, you did not park at the end of the village but up by the farmhouse, where, after paying twenty pounds for a few hours, you could fish shoulder to shoulder with other waistcoats. On approaching the lake, I could not believe what I saw. It was full of fish. They seemed tame, and if you put your foot in the water one or two would come to investigate. Within minutes G had a trout on the bank, and straight after that, another. All over the lake they were being hauled out. But these were not wild brownies, they were kamikaze rainbows. The brown trout was being usurped in this country by an impostor from a Pacific continent, an aggressive import – the rainbow trout. We sent the naive to the dusty plains of the American Midwest in the 1880s and in return we got this synthetic bio-creation, and as their land ate our people, so their fish ate our angling values.

I kept on casting, but was now fishing to a different rhythm, hypnotised by the patterns in the water. It was unnatural. Twenty feet out, my imitation daddy-long-legs floated on the top, one of its legs penetrating the tension of the water's surface. Beneath it I could see jaws opening and then a huge splash. A rainbow gorged the fly and set off on a steroid-fuelled run towards the middle of the lake. I tried to check the reel with my finger, but my skin burnt. My reel had never screamed. But it did so out here, where all the fishing clichés were manufactured for the paying customer. I was down to my backing. Minutes later, when the fish had reversed its dash, it was on the bank. It was too big to kill, so I unhooked it and slipped it into the water. It joined others, fresh from the pens, swimming in a circle, on a macabre merry-go-round, devoid of identity, starved to the point of frenzy.

With these fish came new phrases, glib and without content, ones previously unassociated with trout: 'Four-fish limit', 'double-figure beauty', 'Year-long Trout Fishery'. Trout fishing was meant to be a byword for the noble end of the sport – an art form rather than a pastime, an act of conjuring as opposed to a chuck of chance. The tsars of the dry fly stood no chance. A typically lazy demand had grown for the rainbow, a modern fish for the leisure class; fat and fleshy, tagged, bagged and fit for the freezer age. The old rivers, the Derwent and the Test – and their stocks of brown trout and grayling, that 'Lady of the Stream' – were eclipsed by the arrival of the reservoir: Blagdon, Grafham, Rutland, forged from flooded villages and raped vales, giving birth to these huge deserts of water, rising up like new counties on the map.

A spiral of panic set in. The time in Skye seemed distant once again, like an impossible creation of the mind. I had to connect again, to find a brown trout, to see its fins and spotted flanks and prove to myself that it did exist. The closest place to fish for them was a water called Croxley Hall. There were brownies in the water, but I knew as soon as I heard the name that they could not be wild.

In my head a station announcer's echo reeled off the names on the Metropolitan Line: Harrow-on-the-Hill, North Harrow, Pinner, Northwood Hills, Northwood, Moor Park, Croxley and Watford. The teeth-edge clash of the rails and the electric flash of sparking wheels lighting up the night sky take me out to suburbia. It is a winter evening. Sodium lights light up the carriage, and the green seats are half full of passengers. On the wooden slatted floor are crushed cigarette stubs and pages torn from the evening newspaper. There are pairs of shoes, in line, and above them suited figures, their blank faces staring back at themselves in the grubby windows. A draught runs through the carriage as it speeds across the overground. In one of the seats sits a man, dressed in something other than a suit. He wears Army and Navy chinos; shoes, brown and polished to a perfect reflection; an open shirt; and a green army-issue sweater. On its arms are patches, one of the Royal Signals, one of the Parachute Regiment. Over it all is a grey army greatcoat. His hands are tight and clasped, in brown leather gloves. He does not stare blankly at the windows. In his mind he is somewhere else: driving a motorcycle over the South Downs at sixteen years old to repair the telephone lines; digging a sheep out of a snowy doorway in his first quarters in Catterick; standing on the ramp as the sergeant calls the green lights and shouts 'Go', and he is thrown out into the air, arms crossed on his chest as the line tugs at his chute and it opens. Underneath him is a view of the plains of India, for once silent and orderly, and in his ears is the sound of rushing silence.

The vision is broken by the guard on the train. His deadpan voice calls out the last two remaining stops, 'Next stops Croxley and Watford, where this train terminates.'

The man straightens his back and coughs. Termination. The end of the line. Where did it all go to? It only seems like yesterday that his motorbike was roaring over the hills at the end of the war and he was looking forward to a life of travel and adventure. And soon, he would have to swap all of that, for a desk, for a suit, for an evening paper instead of an imagination. Thirty-three years. India, Burma, Borneo, Malaya, Singapore, France, Germany and finally back to England. The train stops at Watford Junction and the man steps out into the cool air. He coughs but thinks nothing of it. He walks off briskly, his head up and his arms swinging in rhythm next to his side.

And so I looked down upon my father. We lived nearby, in Bushey, on the edge of suburbia. We were his family first but the army ran us close. A soldier like him never leaves his regiment, and if he does he leaves something behind. It is replaced by something new, a sadness, a sense of loss and anger. A bitterness that grows and can be called cancer. It lives within and feeds on unease, on displacement. Because the heart knows that truth is on the side of a wild brown and everything else is chasing rainbows; a new beginning, but futile compared with what has gone before.

Chapter Seven

The camp where we lived in Bushey consisted of roads made up of detached, '50s brick houses, all in the same style, with swing-door garages pitched next to them and steel windows at the front and at the back. In the centre of the estate was a small patch of green surrounded by sets of low-rise flats. We lived at first in a quarter in Harcourt Road and later at one in Turner Road, which led off the former. At the edge of the estate were sets of fields and beyond them was the low rumble of the M1. It was the afternoon of my ninth birthday, St Andrew's Day, 30 November 1975. I was sitting in the living-room of our house and the lights had been turned out. Candlelight lit the room and through it I could see the silhouettes of the houses opposite. They were normally friendly and cartoon-like in appearance but now, with their faces obscured in the dark, their presence was violent and sinister. Amid the comfort and attention of our living-room was a sense of unease and growing insecurity. We were leaving our camp. My father was leaving the army. We were going to Civvy Street. When you've been brought up on army camps they are all you know, and you live as if in a compound, distanced from the civilian world and all its troubles. The civilian world is not one which is portrayed with any sense of sympathy or realism to an army child. A picture is built up of a destitute place, full of poverty and nihilism. Although this world began at the end of our road, and I spent a lot of my time in it, there was still a sense of fear in my mind about what it would be like. If my childhood was a definition of security, imagine that security being enhanced even more by living in a place where you were surrounded by mates, where all the houses had open doors, and the edges of your world were guarded by soldiers. It made you untouchable.

I assumed that Dad's childhood was similar, his father being a soldier like him, too. He would talk occasionally of Jamaica, of going to school in Kingston. He was constantly on the move, developing a deep affection for all the places in which he lived, each one being singled out by a trigger – a song picked up on a foreign long-wave radio station at night; a tobacco tin full of loose coins or stamps; or more everyday things like impromptu billy-can meals of bananas on curry. To stay in one place, to put down roots, was alien to him, unfamiliar; the breaking of a great journey. One of his favourite films was an old silent black-and-white Indian picture about a game of chess. The two players in the film, great rivals, travelled to their respective cities to play matches against one another. The duels would last for days. In the culminating match a deadlock is struck. The moves cannot be resolved. Each player retreats into himself. Both refuse to speak to their curious entourage of family members, cooks and advisers. Still tied on the board, the men part, troubled and distracted. They keep returning but one cannot beat the other. The film ends when one of the players has an epiphany whilst on a train. He smiles and jumps around the carriage. Wild music plays over the speeded up black-and-white stock. He has solved the problem. At the end of the line though, he does not disembark from the train, but merely waits for it to turn around. Once it has done so the closing frame of the film is of the player, having conceded the game by failing to turn up, smiling to himself, looking out over the dusty plain of India. The victory and the true happiness are in his journey. Only when he is playing or moving does he feel any sense of harmony and contentment. I wondered whether my father liked this film so much because it reflected his own life and his wanderlust. If it did then the thoughts he must have had on those last tube journeys must have been more terrifying than they seemed.

And if, that night when Dad stepped off the tube, he had really known the extent of the loss he would feel after leaving, what could he have really done about it? There was nowhere left for him to wander. There was also nowhere for him to go back to except the adopted homeland of his father in Hampshire. To go back beyond that was impossible. His mother had died in 1969, of cancer, too, and there were other doors that for some reason he did not want to go through, or felt he could not. He could not return to his father's house, for it had been sold, not long after he'd died from emphysema in 1973. My father took his pay-off and with his wife of twenty-six years, with half of his young family around him and half of it travelling, he bought a house on the borders of Surrey and Hampshire. The perpetual motion of his life had come to a sudden halt.

Lodge Pond was a small gravel pit of about eight acres, on the road to Bordon in Hampshire. It was surrounded by mile upon mile of pine forest, with a network of foresters' roads cutting through it, running back towards the main road and a pub called the Half Way House. At one end the lake was dammed and the water was deep here, falling away from a gravel shore and the great oaks that grew behind the dam. Small trees and bushes grew all the way down the lake on both sides until it turned into a swampy marsh. It was a significant haven, where people gathered with the single purpose of fishing. It was, almost, like a camp. And now, what is it like? I couldn't tell you, because although I drive past it occasionally, and see the glimmer of the water between the trees I never turn off from the road. I have vivid dreams of it, in which the landscape has changed and the water is full of strange and deformed fish, oversized and grotesque. One day I will go back there, but I cannot say when. The memory of the place is too strong, as if a return there is not needed or even advisable.

Standing in the doorway between two lives. It is a summer's evening in August 1976, and my father and I are fishing at Lodge. Earlier in the day he'd produced the yellow permit. It is the summer before Skye. I can smell the water, surrounded by reeds and couch grass. Tackling up in one of the vacant swims midway down the pond, I can see a small float with a bottle-green stem, a cork body and a brilliantly painted yellow top. For bait we have an old plastic bread bag with the week's collection of stale bread and, as an attractor, an intoxicating bag of ground bait, its brown crumb labelled with a dark-blue block print of a bream on the front of the bag. Our quarry is the gudgeon, a tiny fish of no more than a couple of ounces, which looks as if it is a Home Counties' cousin of the great Russian sturgeon – and the cheerful, perennial English roach, covered in silvery-blue scales with reddish-brown fins and a dark-green back to protect it from the herons.

I can see the fat fluorescent top of the float squatting against the lid of the green, glassy pond, bobbing once and then pulling to one side, before going gradually under. In my father's hand is an old fishing rod. Made of split cane, it has been built for fly fishing, with a short, worn cork handle, aluminium fittings, burgundy whippings and oblique eyed rings. Its tip curves round and the line dances in the water. Under the algae a fish darts from one side of the swim to the other before giving up, and being pulled from the water in a wriggling blur of silver. The roach and the gudgeon follow almost in alternate turns. After a while I am given the rod and told to take over. Darkness is setting in, but rather than a paucity of light there is a brilliant ambient glow about the place, and an echoing stillness. My father stands next to me and is filling his pipe with tobacco. As he smokes, he stares out across the pond towards the woods. This is his doorway between two worlds – the one he had lived in as a soldier, with endless nights sleeping out in the forests of cold-war Europe on military exercises, with a shared brew, piss-taking, maps and laughter; and the one he had now joined as a civilian, a world of gravel drives, bridge, golf clubs, closed doors, privacy without boundary and boredom without limits. A lonely and stifling place. He knocks out his pipe, clears his throat, and says, 'Come on, son, pack up, it's time we were getting home.'

I am standing in a long room at the Phillips auction house in Bayswater, west London. It is February 2000, a few weeks into the new millennium. The room is lit brightly by strip-lights and daylight spots, and the air is controlled by a humidifier. Cases of stuffed and mounted fish line the walls. There is a shoal of perch, static, yet resplendent with their black striped backs and spined dorsal fins – a capsule of time, frozen, their mouths open for prey, immortalised against the reed-stemmed background. There are perfectly restored chub and roach, the work of Cooper and Sons, turning the corpses of fish into something approaching porcelain. A mausoleum for the waters of the last century. Gold letters pick out places whose names evoke the very sense of Jerusalem. A pumphouse on the River Kennet; a stretch of the River Thames above Marlow. In between these works of art stand racks of fishing rods, varnished cane and brass fittings in differing states of repair, and sun-faded canvas and cotton bags hanging on a rail next to them. At the top of the bags with their herringbone stitching are the freestyle labels of gold braid on black silk: 'By Appointment to the Late King George V, to the Prince of Wales 1931–36, Hardy's, the World's Angling Specialist.' Underneath this, a white box reversed out of the black with the simple legend next to it: 'Owner'. The box is blank. Its owner is unknown.

The middle of the room is set with large tables and on them are more rods, stripped of their bags, and numbered in lots. All of their cork handles are black with wear, and chipped by the endless nicking of hooks in their tops at the end of a day's fishing. Under the tables and to one side of the room are dozens of grey packing crates. On them are more lot numbers – 237, 301 – random and unclaimed, and stored inside them are jumbles of tackle. There are old reels without manufacturers' names, the bail arms still smooth after years of oiling and care; cigar boxes, cigarette and tobacco tins, dried milk containers, plastic envelopes with casts and papier-mâché lures; end tackle, tiny hooks beginning to rust, fraying gut and battered leads, improvised line driers made from stubs of card. And wrapped in cloth or kept in old biscuit tins are dozens of floats: cork and quill, reds, greens, black bars on white, wire eyes whipped on, glued and crudely painted. One or two are still attached to a length of line by decaying float rubbers with Thames shot tacked underneath. These are people's lives chucked in a carton, picked over by strangers, dealers mostly, looking for job-lot bargains and the occasional collector searching for one small, significant item. You can see the lives of the dead mapped out from up and down the country, the occasional enamel badge from the Sea Anglers of Blackpool, a Trades Union Fishing Club outside Newcastle, or the Grand Union Canal Association.

I was here at a sale of 'Fishing Tackle and Piscatoriana', but I was neither dealer nor collector. At best I was scavenger. I picked through the boxes at a slower rate than everyone else around me. I was the only one not frantically checking for wear, and writing notes furiously on small pads. I did not laugh and joke with the valuers behind the desk, primly guarding the prize lot of 'A pair of Hardy White Wickham Big Game Sea Fish Reels' – guide price, £15,000 to £20,000. As I wandered round the room and dug through the artefacts a swaying nausea clawed at me. I pictured houses being cleared, rooms being stripped and doors locked for the last time – streets of them, boxed off by red brick and auburn beech hedges, the autumn light pouring in through dirty windows and gathering in dust-filled corners. Carpets have been torn up, patches of underlay stuck to the floor here and there. On the walls are shadows where there used to be pictures or mirrors, and empty, cold fireplaces; the chimneys have been swept and the gas cut off. The outside of the houses are spartan, their windows no longer softened by curtains, but still they retain a cartoon-like appearance. Ordered, and in rows, the streets join in a grid. There are nameplates on small brick walls at the corner of each road: 'Harcourt', 'Mostyn', 'Munro', 'Turner'. The front gardens are overgrown, the concrete driveways broken up by weeds and giant plants. The street lamps flicker on and off. On the edge of this desolation are red triangular signs with the motifs of electric locomotives painted on them and the inscription, WARNING! COMMUTER TRAINS AT WORK! A voice from behind me cuts in, 'Excuse me, mate, are you going to look at that box all day?' I turn, surprised and almost tearful, as if waking from a trance. In my hand is a fishing float, with a bottle-green stem and bright-yellow top. I can't bring myself to place it back in the box, my fingers grip it as if it is a rosary in the hand of a pilgrim.

I cannot fish at this stage. The thought of being next to the water is too terrifying. Fishing is being slowly replaced by a new obsession with old objects, this 'piscatoriana', for want of a better word. All these new things are like clues in a mystery, and I begin to realise that perhaps this is what I am involved in. It is a dialogue with the memory of my dead father, and the more we speak, the more I learn that there were questions I never dared to ask him whilst he was still alive. And these are the ones which trouble me, gnaw at me, dominate my thoughts and drive me further and further back amid the empty boxes. I send off for every catalogue relating to every fishing tackle auction there is. I can no longer afford to bid for items, my unemployment has seen to that, but there is nothing to stop me going to the viewing and perhaps, well, maybe, putting in the odd bid. It's vicarious. You can step outside the room where the viewing is being held and touch the familiar streets full of people just going about their day, passing shop fronts, going in and out of pubs, standing in phone boxes, sitting in cars and on buses.

Motion, going forward, away from the past and into the future. Of course, I daren't tell anyone else about my fear of the water. I must still go fishing at times, but the thought of going by myself, alone, is now too much. At the prospect of it the air is sucked from my belly and the breath shortens in my chest. I realise that I really am expecting to see Dad in these places, and that all of these flashbacks and visions are parts of the conversation we will have. I am distraught at what the outcome will be; how it might change things between us, show a different side to him than the one I cherish. Even in the halls and rooms of the auction houses I can sense his presence, because his story and mine are interwoven with all the stories of the other anglers in the room, the ones picking over the lots, and the ones who left their belongings behind for us. In fishing there is something sacred, hidden. It is certainly a brotherhood, almost Masonic in its curiosity, and the water is witness to its many lost stories.

There was a man, another angler, who lived in north London. He died not so long ago, a few years, maybe. He lived in a fairly large detached house outside Enfield. On his death his widow decided to clear out the places in the house which she exclusively associated with her husband. One of these was the attic. A tackle dealer received a phone call not long afterwards from the widow, asking him to come out to the house. Upon arriving, the man was shown upstairs and left at the foot of the ladder leading into the attic. He climbed the ladder and lifted the hatch. The air was musty and he had difficulty in making everything out as it was fairly dark, despite the light that shone in from a window on one side. Adjusting his eyes he began to focus on the things around him.

The dealer could not believe what he was looking at. He stepped back and peered along the length of the loft space. It was a museum. On the walls were beautifully hand-turned cabinets with green baize backing and onto this, delicately mounted, were sets of floats, exquisite in their presentation. There were sets of rods, polished, hanging in pristine canvas bags on the wall. On tables there were reels, their spools loaded with line but boxed as if new. There were wallets of hooks, artificial flies and plugs and even nets. But there was one thing which didn't add up. None of this tackle looked as if it had ever been used. The man descended the ladder and went to talk to the widow. He mentioned that her husband was obviously a very keen angler. The woman looked at him blankly and said, 'My husband never fished for one hour, let alone one day, during all the time I knew him.'

The widow was adamant, almost angry. She told him that

she just wanted to be rid of the tackle so she could use the attic for storage. She knew her husband and was not about to be told by a stranger what he had or had not done for the past thirty years. The dealer stood and gazed at her, completely lost for words. He agreed to price everything up. It would take days to do it by himself, though, and so he said he would return, take all the tackle away and value it in his shop. The woman said she did not care what he did with the stuff. He could keep it, she just wanted shot of it.

The dealer returned, packed the tackle into a van and took it back to his shop. Several days later, he telephoned the widow. There was about £8,000 worth of gear, he said, and he wanted to know if he could sell it on her behalf. At this point she did start to get angry. Sell it, yes, but keep the money, she told him. The tackle dealer protested but the line went dead. He drove round to the house but was confronted by an even angrier version of the woman who had hung up on him previously. What could he do? Reluctantly, the tackle was gradually sold, and the dealer vowed to return every penny to the widow. He took the money round in cash, in a shoebox. The widow apologised for her anger when they had last met and asked the man in for tea. They sat in her kitchen and he placed the box on the table between them. On lifting the lid off, the widow became angry once more and ordered the dealer out of the house, shoving the box into his hands. There was nothing more he could do. He gave half of the money away to a charity and kept the rest. For days it haunted him. Why had this man built a shrine to fishing and yet never fished? The dealer talked to other tackle shop owners to see if anyone had known the dead man directly. No one could recall him, and of course why should they? Would he be any different to every other angler who comes in to buy tackle? The dealer knew the name of the angler but not his face. He had not seen any photographs of the man in the house. And then, as the days became weeks and the weeks became months, the dealer realised that one of his oldest customers no longer called on his shop. He rang his friends at the other shops and asked if they had seen the man. He'd stopped coming to them as well. Could it be the same man as the angler in the attic? If it was, then why had he bought bait religiously, every week? Pints of maggots, tubs of worms. It seemed the vanished man did fish every week – but when, how and why would remain a mystery. A hidden story which could never be explained, its clues broken down and sold on.

Amongst the mounted perch, chub and roach on the walls of the auction room at Phillips is a curiosity. It is listed in the catalogue as lot number 340, and comes with the following description:

> An extremely rare burbot, the fish mounted in a setting of reeds and grasses against a blue background in a gilt-lined bow-front case with gilt inscription: 'Burbot Eel. 1lb 3oz. Caught by N.R. Lawrance at Matton, River Rye. 18th January 1919.' Case and setting restored and of later date. £1,000 – £1,200.

Under this are three asterisks and the words:

> The burbot is now almost certainly extinct in British waters.

Amid the pastoral comfort suggested by the other fish on sale, the burbot is shocking. It has neither the complete body of a fish, nor that of a serpent, and measures about 20 inches in length. The body is speckled, with pale-yellow spots on the skin, which has the texture of aged brown leather. It is as if it is three fish joined as one. The face is grotesque, the gaping jaw lined with fat lips, and an almost flat head pricked with a small eye which lies virtually on top of the skull. Its gills are veined, reminiscent of the wing of a bat, or the webbed foot of a medieval sea monster. The upper half of its torso is benign, rotund, with unexceptional dorsal, pectoral and lateral fins. The lower half of the fish is one long tail, lined above and below by a pair of spined fins. The tail itself has four sides, in the shape of a diamond. The burbot is an unholy trinity of the cod, the eel and a third unknown fish, far too anonymous to be able to leave its mark on this abomination. At one time the burbot thrived in the rivers and estuaries on the eastern coast of England. It was caught with annoying regularity by anglers fishing for roach or chub on the Ouse, the Rye, the Witham and even as far afield as Yorkshire or Durham. It was also known as the 'eel-pout', possibly on account of its appearance. The flesh of the fish was indigestible, but its black liver was highly prized and viewed as a delicacy.

> The burbot, a freshwater cod with the Latin name *Lota Lota* has not been reported in rivers for ten years. The last is believed to have been caught on the River Ouse in 1969.

For All Those Left Behind

This quote comes from a clipping taken from the *Sunday Telegraph* dated 16 November 1986. The headline states quite simply, 'HUNT FOR BRITAIN'S RAREST FISH'. Beneath it is a photograph of a burbot, freshly killed, its body stiff with rigor mortis and its eyes black. I hold the clipping in my hands. On the reverse of the article is the leading story from the front page. Its headline is also about evolution and survival. It says, 'THREE GET NEW LUNGS IN SECRET TRANSPLANT OPS'. The leader fills three columns and amongst the annual death count from lung disease of 15,000, there is a quote which in truth they could have printed on its own, 'Success is not just about survival; it is about the quality of survival.'

————•—•————

It is the autumn of 1986 and a new meter has replaced the one for the tannoy announcement on the Metropolitan Line. The train is travelling overground but now it stops at Aldershot, Ash Vale, Brookwood, Woking, Clapham Junction and then fast to London Waterloo. It is just after 8 a.m. on a dreary weekday morning, the equinoxial wind lashing the rain against the windows of the carriage. They are misted up but the drops of rainwater can be made out on the other side of the glass, like a thousand Man Ray tears. On the plastic-coated flooring are crushed cigarette stubs and empty styrofoam cups. Crammed into the too-small seats are dozens of people, their shoes similar, their grey suit trousers with the creases washed out in the rain, mackintoshes, and faces hidden behind newspapers. Amongst them sits a man, dressed similarly, in shoes, a suit and mac, the only slight

113

difference being that the shoes are polished to perfection and his trouser creases are sharp. He is annoyed that he had to get into a smokers' carriage. It's not that he hates the smoke – he misses it if he's truthful – but it's been over six years since he was cured of throat cancer and in that time he hasn't even considered smoking. Simple. Black and white. Put his pipe in the bin at Waterloo Station the night he got his first diagnosis.

It's not his regular carriage and with the heat pouring out from the grille under the seat, the place stinks. He sighs and clears the window with his hand. The train runs along the top of an embankment and to the right he can make out a lake. Badshot Lea Ponds. The man closes his eyes. Memories flicker in his head. Maybe he shouldn't have sold those fishing rods after all, but the reality was that his son had left home for good. They wouldn't fish together anymore. But at least they stay in touch. He must remember to send the clipping he saw in the paper yesterday. That would make John smile. The rest of the journey passes slowly. There is no one here he wants to have a conversation with. Soon the man can hear the arrival announcement at Waterloo. He reaches forward, flips open the door and is sucked out into the throng – a huge procession, glum and resigned, heading for the exits.

Chapter Eight

The pike is prehistoric in appearance and unlike any other freshwater fish. Its size alone sets it apart. A large pike will have a head as large as a human's and a body almost as long. Its jaws are lined with molars that curve inwards to trap any prey and it has gills like the wings of a rook. The roof of its mouth is lined with row upon row of razor-sharp teeth that can serrate with the slightest touch. The flanks are mottled, normally a green colour with creamy blotches rising up to its back. Its fins are a muddy brown. The tones of its scales change to blend with its surroundings, so it can vary from bright green to a brick red in appearance. The mouth is flat and elongated and eyes, like no others, seem to have been pushed into the head. They sit angrily, one-way windows above a chamber of horrors. A small pike – and by this I mean one of under six or seven pounds, big enough to hang over the sides of an average dining table – is known as a jack. This is the court jester to the king and queen of the river. Jacks are incessantly greedy, feeding constantly in a frantic race to reach a size where they can become a feared predator rather than fearful prey. But this greed has its risks and occasionally an angler can come across something washed up which looks like the beginnings of some bizarre occult ritual. As two jacks pass each other, with no more than a cursory glance, they will turn and snatch. The jaws of one will engulf the head of the other. The teeth then lock in and cannot move. The two pike are now one, unable to free their bodies, only locking further into fatal majesty with each lunge, completing a slow circle of terror. The Union Jack.

When you tell people that you are going fishing, their eyes glaze over. You carry on anyway, describing where you're going and losing yourself in anticipation of just being there. Meanwhile, whoever you were talking to has left the room. When you tell people that you are going pike fishing, the reaction is different. For if fishing has the popular image of a pastime carried out by dull people in bad weather, the pike has a more engaging image, one based on fear and fascination, which pervades all corners of non-angling society. In either case you'll be avoided ever after, either for being someone who has regressed beyond redemption, or for being slightly unsettling; an urban fake with poacher's blood.

I'm not saying that I'm either of these, but I'm sure there's a bit of both in all of us who fish, just as there is some Wodehouse and Hemingway – the weekend escapee who responds to the allure of an exclusive trout water, or the tube passenger who nurtures the desire to go gun running and marlin fishing off Cuba. But if anything, the pike holds a strange power over me and in the last few years it has been getting stronger. My first encounter with one saw memory become myth.

The afternoon wore on and it started to rain very gently, that gauze of summer drizzle that cuts the warmth out of the air and promises evening. My father suggested that we move to a more sheltered spot on the river in case the rain got worse. We got back to the car and drove off down the road, following the course of the river. After a while the river swept off to our left across a field. In the middle of the field was a glade of trees which grew into a wood. The river flowed right into it. Pulling the car onto the side of the road and tucking it against the stone wall, my father brought us to a halt. He fetched the tackle from the back and we set off across the field, sticking to its edge, round the foot of the dry-stone wall. Soon we came to the wood. Underneath the canopy of trees it was as if someone had switched the lights out. It was dark and suddenly you were aware of the noise of the water as it echoed around its natural chamber. We weren't fishing for trout anymore. The mood had changed.

My father put his finger to his lips and unhooked the small gold spinner from the butt ring of the rod. With a deft flick of the wrist, the lure landed about twenty yards downstream under a tree. The retrieve was quicker than it had been for the trout and every so often Dad would jerk the line or shake the tip of the rod to make the lure imitate an injured fish. He fished in this manner for about another half an hour or so, creeping up and down the bank, using the trees for cover. It was now growing dark outside the wood as well as within it. Just the time at which we would surely catch. Suddenly, from behind us, a branch snapped underfoot and we turned to see a bellicose man, tweeded up from head to foot, carrying a shotgun. He demanded to know what we were doing fishing his stretch. He had his nets to lay. He didn't want 'some interferin' types' spoiling the river. Dad humoured him but Tweeds wouldn't drop it. An argument started. I was conscious of the gun, but never believed it would be used.

Whatever happened next is a complete blank. I remember that feeling of being hunted, of locking the door of the car, the figure standing at the edge of the trees, returning my gaze as I looked back. I can still feel the fear; the security of our holiday being gatecrashed by this sinister figure. We didn't return to the river for a couple of days and we never went back to the wood. In that short stretch of river, under dark mossy banks, a pike lay sulking, hugging the roots of the submerged trees. I have been trying to catch it for my father ever since.

The first one I brought home wasn't even one I had caught myself. It was one that had been captured and killed by a T.W. Yates on 23 February 1928. It weighed 20 lb 8 oz. It was mounted at a taxidermist's in Paddington. Its journey is unknown after that. Then I came face to face with it in Bonham's auctioneers seventy years later and in an impulsive fit of desire parted with £1,000 for it. From the moment it arrived home in the back of a cab it ruled the house. It had been dead for decades, but I still checked it every now and again out of the corner of my eye as I went up the stairs. Was that a fin that moved? Was that an eye that flickered in my direction? It soon became the moose in *Twin Peaks*, talking to me on a regular basis and staying schtum whenever anyone else was in the house. I winced when people made jokes at its expense, anticipating the obvious doom that would soon befall them. Most visitors treated it with respect, intuitively aware of its powers as a talisman of horror. It watched over our meals and filled with room with a solemn glory. As the weeks went on I began to wonder exactly what it was people meant when they asked whether anyone had ever been taken by a pike. It was not as simple as summer bathers losing a foot or a hand in the shallows as they strayed too near the reeds – it was deeper and wilder than that. It meant waking in the middle of the night, the sodium glow of the London sky lit like a cauldron outside, and knowing that nailed to the wall downstairs was a fish under whose spell I had fallen. It implored me to pack my rods into the back of the car immediately and set off into the darkness.

G and I had been doing this for a couple of seasons now without any tangible success. The more the pike eluded us, the more tantalising the search became. I'd fished for pike in my childhood at two places – Badshot Lea Ponds and Frensham Great Pond – and I knew that it would be to there that I would have to return. Our trips to Frensham Great Pond for tench had rewarded us beyond expectation and although it was a massive water which could be fished for weeks with little to show for it, I also knew that this was where we would make the connection. It was becoming increasingly apparent to me that part of me was seeking another quarry: the answer to a mystic riddle. Where the search was leading me as part of this process was something I didn't question. There were waters that felt right and there were waters which did not. Each time I fished one of the former another clue would emerge, another lesson would be spelt out. They appeared regularly enough and I was utterly unconscious of them, but after a while they began to sketch out a pattern which, although random, was quite definite in its rhythm. I began to realise that if I pursued the silent voice with sufficient conviction, then soon enough it would speak.

The pike was first introduced into Frensham Great Pond in or around 1860. It decimated the farmed stocks of trout within years. Other species such as the perch, rudd and tench survived more easily, probably due to their ability to shoal up against attack. However, none of the fish, not even the pike, could withstand the netting that took place on a regular basis every five years up until the end of the nineteenth century. They would then be sold on to fish markets, in London mostly. Coarse fish were in demand then; they were fresher than their saltwater cousins, who would arrive twice as ripe. A pike caught in the evening could be on the wagons in the Catholic quarters and Jewish ghetto by the following morning. The netting carried on until the fishing rights were sold by the Ecclesiastical Commissioners to the landlord of the neighbouring inn, the White Horse. To fish it thereafter you needed to be in credit at the bar there. G and I arrived on 29 November 1998 in my diesel-powered white horse by way of the fishmonger and the pub. It was about 3.30 p.m. when we pulled up in the car park above the pond. A blue sky was reflected in the waves that cut across the lake like an undiscovered ocean. It was cold. Dog walkers turned their collars to the breeze and their thoughts to home as we unloaded our gear and changed into more layers of clothing. We walked down along the hotel bank and pitched up in a couple of the swims under the cover of the trees. At the hotel end the water was in the lee of the wood and the surface was completely calm. The scene was one of peace; the approaching dusk was ushered in gently by the thin light of a winter's afternoon. I couldn't envisage encountering any self-respecting pike at this time, so tackled up just the one rod for perch and, casting it out, sat back to enjoy the rays of the sun as it sank reluctantly behind what had once been the White Horse Inn.

I was blasé, to the point of overconfidence. This was a day that felt right. Not because of the conditions now but because of the evening they precluded. I was waiting for the switch to be flicked and for The Pond to come to life. G was in a swim next door, his usual impatient self, driven only by the need to catch fish. Having three young children, he needed a justification for his absence and anything other than instant results made him agitated. This made him my ideal fishing partner – reliably silent and eventually sullen, his mood becoming a distant chorus chanting a bass litany of Gregorian proportions. And the bastard never brought his own coffee. Having polished off the remains of our one flask, G declared himself restless again, and set off round to the sluice in search of jacks with a plugging rod. We had moved both sets of rods into one swim by this time, under some tall silver birches and hemmed in by holly bushes. The last of the walkers had gone and we had the pond to ourselves. The water was golden as the sun sank and left its burnt red glow upon the advancing night sky. There was life all around. The birds sang as if it was the last day on earth and a hatch of midges danced above the water. In the leaves up and down the bank I could hear the scurrying of voles and robins as they searched in vain for scraps of food. Dogs, quarantined in the kennels not far away, had fallen silent for the first time in the afternoon. Lights from a house in the wood on the far corner of the pond glowed like windows onshore. I felt like a castaway again, circumnavigating the habits of a normal Sunday, gathering exhibits as I went, distilling them in imaginary victuals and labelling them in ink.

It was virtually dark when G returned, asking if there was more coffee. It was my turn to be sullen as I had fallen into a cold trance. The advance of night had brought the first whisper of frost to the ground and now all life had been chilled into silence, with the exception of the dogs and foxes, who exchanged barks intermittently. Their voices echoed round the woods and bounced off the water, disorientating me. We baited up for the long wait. Half herrings were hooked, tied and chucked into the blackness. A distant splash was all the indication we had of where the cast had landed. Wading back through the water, the rods tucked behind us, the bail arm off, paying line out – the traps were set. We sat and watched the water turn a silvery blue as a late harvest moon rose across us. About an hour in, we heard voices and footsteps approaching down the bank. Two figures came closer, their progress marked out by the bouncing tips of their cigarettes. We stood up and dug our hands into our pockets. They stopped behind us, sucked their teeth, and asked us if we'd had anything. After a minute or two of whispers they slunk off down the bank in the direction of the road.

G and I were busy taking bets on who they were and where they'd come from when my rod's buzzer sounded. Not a run, just a nudge, enough to make it bleep a couple of times. My heart started to race, setting my adrenalin on its marks and shortening my breath. It knocked again and then picked up speed. I crouched over the rod and let the line run out over my fingers. After a few seconds I turned over the bail arm, tightened up the slack and whacked the rod back over my shoulder. It kicked before I could even raise it vertically and the old cane bent against the cool glow of the sky.

The fish was about forty yards out to the left of the swim and in front of the old reed bed. It ran and ran. The clutch couldn't check its progress, so to fight it I stepped off the bank and climbed into the water. It was warmer than the air as the pressure wrapped my waders against me. The fish was beginning to tire but was still fighting doggedly. Every now and again it would shake its head and the rod would judder from side to side whilst the line gave out a high-pitched twang. G had followed me out with the net and the two of us stood on the edge of the tree line, bathed in light, two figures on the edge of the civilised world. The fish hit the surface about twenty yards out in an explosion which broke our reverent silence. 'Jesus,' we said in unison.

I got the pike's head up and pulled it the last yard over the net. It kicked and turned again as it sensed the mesh – years of instinct reminding it of the prospect of an undignified end in London's fish markets. But it was tired and had nowhere to go other than the folds of the net. Once in, G lifted the arms of the net, I clicked off the bail arm and we walked back through the water to the bank of the lake. A shout of triumph split the night, heralding the end of a wait that seemed longer than its two years. Turning the fish over on its back I slid the index finger of my right hand in under the flesh of the gills and cocked the pike's jaws. My hooks were out in a second but an older bait and trace protruded from the opening in the stomach. The trace of this one had been severed just inches further up and the hook was set too deep to free. After weighing and taking a photo of it, I laid the fish back in the water. Despite the older hooks set deep in its belly I was not going to give it the last rites and blessing of a brass-headed priest. I was returning it to its lair to heal itself and hunt once more against the shroud of a winter's night.

There was a pub up the road called the Mariners Inn. It was here in 1855 that an inquest was held over the body of a child who had lived for only three hours before being drowned in the pond. The verdict of wilful murder against persons unknown was passed. When you drive over the bridge and park outside the pub on a winter's night it is easy to imagine what the surrounding landscape would have been like 150-odd years ago. The grim journey, by foot from the pond to the inn, would have taken them only half an hour, and the only sound they would have heard as they pushed open the door of the inn would be the one we heard now, the sound of the river running under the stone bridge. As we entered the pub, the fire roared, but all the tables were empty. A man appeared from behind the bar and asked what we were drinking. He was tall and had to stoop under the low-slung beams of the roof. G got them in whilst I went to clean up in the toilets. I'd broken the third finger on my left hand the day before, and the evening's fishing hadn't improved it. The cold had left all my fingers swollen and this one doubly so. It was turning black and my wedding ring cut into my skin – a magical symbol, never to be taken off. Back at the bar I joked that the finger would have to come off before the ring and that I would wear the silver band and the bones round my neck forever. G and I emptied our glasses and talked excitedly, passing our own verdict on the night's proceedings. We'd hunted down one of Lucifer's own children and snared him with the symbol of Christianity. But there was nothing sacred about the occasion; if anything, with each passing hour on the banks of the lake, the night had become more and more pagan.

There is a vacuum between Christmas and New Year. You've over-socialised, squared off your eyes in front of the television, and developed a liking for port. The sofa, the curtains, the cushions and even the carpets threaten to envelop you. I picked up the phone and called G. He was going crazy, nothing new in 'Rochester Castle', and within seconds we'd convinced each other that another pike trip was the only option. Trying to get bait was a tall order in itself. All the fish markets were closed and the harbours were silent. In the back of my freezer I found the blackened head of a trout and a frozen lamprey. G fared better, stating that you could buy anything in Kentish Town with the right connections. I tried hard to assimilate the link between mountain bikes, handguns and grade-one herring but gave up and had to agree. There were some good boozers up there, too. The best one stood boarded up at the corner of Anglers Lane and Kentish Town Road. In its front window was a yellowing piece of paper giving details of a fishing-club outing to Ireland by coach. Perhaps they'd never made it back. The next day we were off and running down the A3. We never took motorways on public holidays; it was one of our unwritten rules, stay off the beaten track.

Frensham was deserted, more so than ever by the time we arrived. It was midwinter and the light was already failing. It was about three o'clock. The bare branches of the trees and the blackened, wet leaves underfoot combined to give that smell of stale damp that signifies that time of year. The hotel bank would offer no shelter now, so we crossed over the fence and into the conservation area, where there were two swims adjacent to one another. The reed beds had died down completely and a wren flitted in and out of the stumps that poked out of the water. In the early summer, these same reed beds had been alive with spawning fish, crashing against the stems all day and all night. Now, in the crystal clear water, it was hard to see a single sign of life.

We baited up, me with a lamprey section and G with his holy herring. The light hadn't altered for an hour, twilight was suspended. Broken sunlight lit up the surface of the water on the other side of the pond. The bullrush beds gleamed like silver in the unexpected light. Soon fat drops of rain fell into the water like lost sovereigns and within seconds the opposite perimeter of the bank, less than half a mile away, was invisible, gone in the squall. The rain lashed down in stair rods. It continued like this for only minutes and then the cloud was split by a giant ray of sunlight and a dazzling rainbow that rose out of the centre of the lake. Our buzzers stayed silent but the red lights on the front lit up sporadically as the baits were rocked in the current. Out in front of us was where the trench was at its deepest and the banks either side of it made the water very shallow. Our baits must have been lying on top. It had been cold before the storm but now the air was bitter, stinging the skin on my face. A moon had risen swiftly and was almost full. It shone above us, sitting like a giant stellar invader over the tips of the spruces on the hill above the east bank. It was mottled and it seemed so close. Closer than London, than pavements and front doors, and the call for last orders. I watched its slow progress in its reflection on the water. G and I didn't talk, couldn't talk, above a whisper. It was time to pull in our baits and acknowledge the stalemate before us. We packed up our gear slowly, slower than we realised, arms and hands numb, our minds slurred like vodka waiting to freeze.

The motor was only about twenty five yards away but there was a good hour between lifting our lines and turning the key in the frozen lock of the driver's door. The light in the ranger's office had long since gone out. I drove the car across the gravel path towards the road. The windscreen was completely misted up and, sticking my head out of the open window, my heart sank. The metal gates were chained and padlocked shut. I shone the full beam on them thinking that maybe somehow that would be enough. I turned off the engine, swore and got out of the car. With a rope and many revs we could probably get them off their hinges, but we had neither. The route out either side of the gate was fairly clear apart from a few stakes which had been driven into the ground but a pair of trenches had been dug out and these would swallow the wheels of any car. G and I looked at each other. We had just about enough bait to make it through the night, and we could walk to the pub in the meantime to get well stocked.

I looked back over my shoulder and in the distance could make out waves in the moonlight lapping onto the shore. The yule tide washing up against the devil's punchbowl. We wouldn't catch anything that night. The pike were spooked and in hiding. Simultaneously, G and I started kicking at the stakes, rocking them in their shallow foundations. We quickly had enough to make a pontoon by throwing them into one of the trenches and covering it over with leaves and twigs. I reversed the car back through the trees, pulled up the handbrake, slammed down the accelerator, dropped the handle and the white horse shot out and over the ditch into the road. I dipped the beam, G got into the passenger seat and we set off to find streetlamps and sanity.

It was the last day of the season. G couldn't get away from work, but as I'd been laid off and paid out, I could afford to indulge myself for a while. I rang G in the morning to see if he'd changed his mind but the answerphone was on. I replaced the receiver without leaving a message. I would fish alone today. That was how I wanted it, for once. The atmosphere of the lake had really begun to possess me. The pike symbolised a force and a feeling which I felt compelled to confront. By hunting them down I had begun to erase the eerie presence which hung over me whenever I fished there. I felt I'd done enough to lay the tweed ghost of my childhood to rest with pike after pike over the winter months. In other words I was looking for a sign. A sign that it was all right now; that my father and I were fishing side by side once more. The spectres would have gone and our conversation would be weightless, about nothing, wonderfully immaterial and frivolous.

We'd discovered a new place to fish at Frensham. Along the south-eastern shore of the pond ran a vast bed of tall reeds. They grew about eight or nine feet above the water line. Towards the corner of the pond there was a narrow break in the bed, no more than two and a half, maybe three feet in width. You could wade out from the shore along this corridor and eventually come to a clearing. In the middle of this a platform had been built on old scaffolding poles. A makeshift ladder allowed you to climb up onto the boards. From here, you could cast across the bay and along the front of the reed beds. G and I had fished here and nowhere else for most of the winter – it was gloriously isolated and cut off from the bank, which was hidden from view by a bend in the reed corridor.

I passed through the trees and bushes until I reached the break in the reed bed. I climbed into the water and carried my gear above my head and out to the platform. It was a grim March day, with a leaden sky and a wind gusting up to fifty miles an hour. The water, normally crystal clear, was churned up. In the wind the reed stalks brushed together in a ju-ju clatter. Even though the forecast had said the temperature would be around eight or nine degrees, the wind chill cut it way below this. I only had one rod with me, so I quickly tackled it up and waited for the gusts to abate before casting out. Waves broke over the front of the platform. The colour of the water was North Atlantic gunmetal grey, with white horses riding the length and breadth of the lake.

There wasn't even a sun to set, on this most auspicious of days. I consoled myself with the thought that the next time I returned here, midsummer would have transformed this inland ice floe into an Ophelian paradise. By dark I'd had two runs and two jacks, fighting like barracuda in the waves. I could make out their shapes by the silvery flashes of their flanks as they rose out of the depths, clutching the baits in their jaws. I was convinced that this was the day I would hook into the monster. The conditions grew more inhospitable as the night fell around me. I would stay until something happened. It got too cold to count the hours, and the lake became more and more desolate. I felt the years speeding backwards beyond time. It was soon pitch black. I took my hat off and listened. The reed stems, many of them broken off in the gale, swished around. They sang like midwest telegraph lines in the desert. The water slapped against the underneath of the boards on the platform. I felt cut off, the anchor rope severed, as I drifted in my imaginary skiff across the centuries. Faces and voices passed before me, shrieks and cries blistered my eardrums, hands and arms rose out of the water, gesturing helplessly. What was happening here, I would never understand, not in a dozen seasons, and I was beginning to realise that I was only scratching the surface of solitude. I drank it up, in huge gulps, filling my lungs with the primitive air.

I sat, my knees pulled up to my chest, my back hunched over the top of them, peering out into the night, raging against my demons, knowing this time and the many more beyond it would bring no more than another onslaught of questions and silent replies.

Chapter Nine

The herring are not in the tides as they were of old;
My sorrow! for many a creak gave the creel in the cart
That carried the take to Sligo town to be sold,
When I was a boy with never a crack in my heart.
'The Meditation of the Old Fisherman', W.B. Yeats

I was in the bar of Blooms Hotel in Dublin. It was a Wednesday night or Thursday morning in January 1993. There'd been an argument, a flashpoint of some kind, everyone was so drunk the spark had been forgotten. The air hung with violent reproach. Something had been said, something had passed which could not be ignored. It had changed things between us but we were so gone that none of us could remember what it was. The barman cleared our empty glasses and duly replaced them with full ones. Steve was trying to calm Margaret and me down. We had a bond, because I was the spit of her brother and she the spit of my sister. This made us mates and drinking partners on the odd occasion. Tonight, though, something had gone wrong and our words flew back and forth like night tracer. The bar couldn't empty, it was just us and the house lights. Talking about family. Shouting about loss.

O'Leary was the surname, but for years I'd known him only by his Christian name of Allen. He was my father's cousin. Each March the card would arrive without fail – a green four-leafed clover, sometimes with gold trim – to be greeted by silence. I'd always wondered who was sending them, what they meant. The silence was frightening. Not much made my father brood but this simple gesture seemed to quieten him more than anything. It was as if there was a conflict going on within him, one that he did not want us to be aware of. All day I would avoid him and he us. I must have asked once who the card was from. I must have been told. I never asked again. It was like a door in our house which was permanently locked. I knew people lived on the other side of it. I knew they did the same things as us, at the same times. I was acutely aware of their presence. But I had never seen nor heard them.

And then once a year, just at the point that I'd forgotten about it all, that card would be slipped under the door. Only one person could open it, my father. It was addressed to all of us as 'the family', the only letter which ever was, but that made no difference. Afterwards, when it stood opened on the table, when there was no one in the room, I would sneak a look to decipher the code. Invariably, all it would say would be 'Happy St Patrick's Day, love from Allen, Pat and family'. It was confirmation that those were indeed voices that I heard on the other side of the door; that I wasn't wrong in wondering who they belonged to or what they were saying. It was another side to my father which I knew nothing about.

For years it had been a mystery that I'd been eager to solve. Now, years later, I was hours from knocking on the door and seeing who was behind it.

It had started the day before Dad died, when we were taking it in turns to read to him. He stared out in front of him, his eyes opening and closing at intervals, drifting in and out of sleep. His breathing was loud and uneven, his lungs full of fluid but his mouth dry. It was just him and me in the room. Outside you could hear the odd passing car and inside the ticking clock, echoing off the Formica of the bedside table, and my self-conscious voice trying desperately to fill the space with some kind of comfort. He tapped my arm and gestured for me to give him some water. Closing his eyes again, he said, 'Go to Dublin. See Allen. It will do you good.' He never mentioned it again after this. I didn't think about it much either.

It hardly seemed important at the time. You could have told me that the house was burning down and it would not have registered. I was watching and waiting, almost too tense to acknowledge anything. I filed it away in my mind along with everything else I'd seen and heard that day. I knew I would want to pore over it later, but then I just had to get through it.

I was now staring at the address on a scrap of paper I'd been carrying around in my wallet. The argument in the bar had been broken up by the arrival of a bloke, fully bearded and carrying a staff. Jesus Christ, obviously, to us in our state; to the rest of the world, he was simply the singer from Hothouse Flowers. It was 3 a.m. at another hotel on the path of excess. I tucked the paper square back into my wallet and staggered towards the lift, my reflection threatening me in the mirrored walls, and then towards my bed, the room tilting, the bed spinning, my heart beating loudly in my splitting head and my belly filled with a mission. It had now been about a year since Dad had died. When I'd been given the chance to return to Dublin for work I'd jumped at the opportunity. I could go to the International and to O'Daid's, where I coveted the brushed mirror sign for Andrews Whiskey. I could sit in bars and talk to strangers about anything and nothing. It could be a holiday, and how I wanted one.

The next day, I was on one of those lost lunches where the whole city had seemed reluctant to return to work. The afternoon sun softened as it shone through the windows and onto the red-topped tables. The smoke from the bar looked like incense in the pale light. I felt strangely holy, from the Day-glo embrace of a couple of pints of the blackest stout. The words came back to me and filled my head. 'Go to Dublin. See Allen,' and I was off. Thinking about that weekend. Of all the grief. Of seeing my family in such pain. I welled up, took a slug of my drink, gritted my teeth and knotted my gut. Not here, not in a pub, in daylight, in a foreign city. That was too desperate. I put down my glass and walked out, past St Stephen's Green and down towards the Liffey.

It had only taken a phone call, to my Uncle Terry, my father's brother, to find out the O'Learys' address. I'd intended to make another, to tell them I was coming. But that would have given them the option to say they'd be out. I ate a full breakfast first, with double helpings of black pudding, peeling the rind off just like Dad used to. My stomach fought with my head for urgent attention. Still pissed. I could have eaten six platefuls. I swilled it down with cups of tea and read the *Irish Times*. Small ads on the front page invited me to buy a hat or invest in a timeshare in Connemara. I checked my limbs for signs of growth. I felt like the man in Kafka's *Metamorphosis*. Waking up to a changed world, a new identity. The sunshine beat off the river as I walked across the bridge and up past the post office. The air was clear, the sky a sheer blue, with a wind whipping down from the docks and pushing everyone indoors. For the first half a mile or so it could have been any European capital with its chain stores and traffic. After a while the road narrowed and the shops seemed to become less confident and brash. I kept on, towards the signs for Phibsborough, feeling as if I was reaching the real part of the city, not the postcard square mile which was held out to most visitors. I'd memorised the route and knew that as soon as I'd reached Dalymount Park I'd have gone too far. A huge building dominated the road, a turret belching white smoke into the sky. The hospital. I was near.

And then, there I was, in a tiny terraced street, no more than six or eight houses, everything washed clean and gleaming by the overnight rain. I knocked on the door of one of them. A woman opened it and looked puzzled at the stranger on her doorstep.

'I'm Ted Andrews' son, John.'

She looked at me again and a smile of recognition broke out on her face. 'It's Teddy's boy, John, Teddy's boy – I don't believe it.' And with that I was ushered in, and given the best seat in the house, at the kitchen table, next to a giant teapot. A fire was in the grate and an empty dog basket sat next to it, full of white dog hair. Allen was blind and so no dog in the house meant he was out. The woman was Pat O'Leary, his wife. For the next two hours I sat rooted to my chair as a procession of distant cousins came in and out, asking me how I was, as if we'd known each other since birth and I'd last seen them only at breakfast. I was fed cheese on toast and given more tea.

There was more commotion and in came Allen, his guide dog licking my knees and its tail beating the door. I stood up and shook Allen's hand. Before I could loosen the grip he had reached up and was feeling my face with his other hand. In and around my eye sockets, down my nose and round my chin. He couldn't miss my ears. Jugs. 'He looks like his father.' What Allen couldn't see was that I had my own tears. Ones of surprise and joy. The house was full of people. One of them pulled up another chair for Allen and he sat down opposite me. 'Now tell me about your brother and sisters. I remember them on the lawn at Liss, what are they doing now?' I explained their various paths and relationships, the names of their own families. 'Get the box down from the attic,' he said. Another member of the household was despatched upstairs and brought down a cardboard box with envelopes in it. Inside were photographs, so old they had to belong to the previous century. They were pictures of my great grandmother and great grandfather. Allen passed them to me. 'These are yours now.' He explained who they were. I had been emptied of emotion, drained raw by rush after rush of revelation and shock. Now a ghost stared at me from the sepia print. It was the face of my father in the face of his grandmother.

We talked some more, the same talk, small talk, on the same side of the wall, in the same room. I discovered half the family were boat builders, that I had a thousand cousins called Foley in Finsbury Park. I discovered that Allen was involved in the preservation of the local canal. He was a man of water. From a family of water. And I sat in his kitchen and felt as if it were my own. But at the same time I felt like such an impostor, an impossible fraud, a genealogical tourist. I wanted to stay but felt I had to go. I turned down the offer of a bed for a night, told them I'd phone before I left and walked back out into the arms of my foreign city.

It is 1920. The town of Ennis in County Clare is in the west of Ireland, which at this time is still one nation. One nation torn to ribbons by feuding and struggles for power and destiny. There are many armies and forces in this land, and within them many parts. There is the Irish Republican Brotherhood, the forerunner of the IRA; there are the Irish Volunteers and the Irish Citizen Army. There is the British Army with its famous southern regiments such as the Dublin Fusiliers and the Connaught Rangers. There is the Royal Irish Constabulary and the Auxiliaries, formed from the tougher elements of the Black and Tans. And there are the people, all of whom come from large families with divided loyalties. Between them they are engaged in a fight for supremacy against one another, following the orders of their commanders. A quote from Robert Kee's *Ireland – A History* sums up the situation that everyone lived with:

> By late 1920, Sinn Fein's attempt to assert the Irish
> Republic politically and the British government's

attempt to solve the Irish problem had deteriorated virtually into a guerrilla warfare between two increasingly vicious bands of armed men, the 'Tans' – a term colloquially often extended to cover the Auxies too – and the IRA. The Irish people were in the middle . . . As in 1798, reprisal and counter reprisal followed each other in a cycle of apparently unending horror.

On a street in this town of Ennis there is a house. It is made of stone and has small windows and a black slate roof. A chimney stack sits on top of this and from it a faint wisp of smoke curls into the night sky. It is one of many houses, in one of the many streets, that make up this town in the west. From a downstairs window there is a yellow light. Within the room from which this light comes sit two young people, a woman and a man. The woman's name is Lily Foley, aged nineteen, one of nine children born in the house. She is trained as a nurse. The man's name is Thomas Edward Andrews, known as Teddy, aged twenty-one, one of six children born in the county of Dublin in the east of the island. Since the death of his mother in childbirth he has been trained at the Royal Hibernian Military School in Dublin to be a soldier. They sit and talk and smoke, their conversation the same as every courting couple there has ever been. As the evening continues the ashtray fills and the air thickens until the yellow light is almost silver. In the other houses in the street, and across the town, lights are gradually put out and a darkness descends on the place. The silver light from the Foley's house continues to shine on. Inside there is now talk of a different kind, born of clandestine circumstance, from a romance under siege. It is of a wedding planned for later that year and the new life that there will inevitably be afterwards, of postings in foreign cities, of flight and a new home together, away from all of this.

It was a Tuesday night in November 2000. I was in the bar of the Roisin Dubh in Gurteen, County Sligo. It was empty but for two children, an old man watching the television, myself and Deborah. Outside, the yellow glow of the street lamps made the road shine in the darkness. The smell of peat and coal blew up and down the street. Sitting with our backs to the window we could sense the damp pawing at the walls. The interior had been painted a dark blue and had been ordained with sets of pictures and photographs. Had you taken a photograph of it yourself you would have had an image of snug cosiness on a winter's evening – family and regulars at the bar and a couple in the corner.

Above our table stood another man. On the face of it, it was a painting of a soldier, dressed in a green uniform, with freshly cut hair, proud in his peaked cap, with a brown and brass belt set and laced boots. In his hand was a rifle. *I was conscious of the gun, but never believed it would be used.* This was no ordinary portrait, though, it was a tribute to Michael Collins, self-styled leader of the Irish Free State Army. In the corner was a doorway which led through to a back bar, full of tables, chairs and portraits of other Irishmen, dressed casually in trousers, shirts and informal jackets. They were equally as proud as the oil-painted emperor in the other room but in their hands were fiddles, drums, pipes and flutes. I was on my first pint of the evening. The yellow animated man on the Tayto crisp packet smiled at me. The bars on the gas heater placed by the door flickered and phutted.

The bar started to fill at around 10 p.m. By this time I'd had another and a fug was taking the chill off the air. A procession of men and women, both young and old, came through the door of the pub. All of them greeted one another on entering and went to stand by the bar. In their hands were cases of black or brown leather, firmly shut with clasps and straps. A couple of feet in length, they were set down and tucked under stools whilst the chatter rose to a low hum. A man with dark hair and a beard came in, wearing an ill-fitting anorak that looked as if it had been hastily thrown on. Under his arm was a large plastic bag. He did not put this down, but accepted a pint as it was hoisted over heads and placed in his spare hand. He took a swig from the glass and emptied half in one go. Glancing around the bar he shuffled off into the other room.

I was going fishing the next morning. I drank slowly, knowing that I wouldn't want to share my boat with a hangover, however fresh the air would be. There were giant pike in Temple House Lake. The water stood on the shores of a derelict castle that was once occupied by the Knights Templar, giving the subsequent name to the estate of which the Georgian and Victorian Temple House was the splendid centrepiece. Its vast lake stretched over a mile and a half in length. The shores were fringed by farm land and ancient forest, the water lapping over beaches of broken limestone or merging into huge beds of reed mace. It ran fairly shallow, averaging around six feet in depth with the exception of the water off the tip of the island at the southern end, where the floor shelved away to the deeps. Here the water was inestimable, dropping anything from twenty to sixty feet. Due to the excessive rainfall the lake was in flood and its level was at least four feet higher than usual. I had seen it upon our arrival at the house, in the gathering dusk. Walking round the edges where the surface was still, the water broke and a bow wave rolled out from almost under our feet, under the bank. I put up a lure rod and worked the bay but with the approaching black night came nothing except the cry of rooks echoing off the walls of the old castle.

I looked at my watch. It was gone eleven. My glass was nearly empty and Deborah was asking if I wanted another. I nodded and said I'd get them on the way back from the toilet. I walked into the other room and through the door of the gents. The smell of stale urine and bleach caught my throat but was soon replaced by the rush of cool air which came through an open window above the stalls. It was silent. I coughed and the sound echoed off the tiles. With a shove of the door I was out in the bar again. The bearded man watched me as I crossed the room. He was standing with his back to an empty grate. I ordered another pint of Guinness and a lemonade. The barman took a plastic bottle, unscrewed the top and poured the contents into a glass and placed it in front of me. The liquid was red. I looked puzzled and the barman tapped his fingers on the label. I smiled. It said, 'Red Lemonade' and he looked at me as if there was no other kind. Our bar emptied quickly as the men and women carried their cases through next door, leaving a collection of dead pint and short glasses massed on the bar top. Deborah and I followed.

The men and women were seated in a large circle. On the

edges of it, posted into a nook of a corner was the eldest woman. The men were all dressed similarly, in shoes and boots, trousers and jackets with shirt collars, some knotted with ties and some unkempt. Under the chairs and to one side were the empty cases, their red and orange velvet linings lying open. Like giant mussel shells on the sand. The moment a tune started the atmosphere changed. Not only that but the small pub seemed to fill as if by magic. More and more people came. All the seats were taken. One of the players would lead by picking out the melody on the steel strings of the banjo and within seconds the flutes and fiddles were in time. The man with the beard knelt over a bodhrán and his hand dealt the rhythm. This was not music; that was too simple a term for it. It was at once a wail and a whisper, *faces and voices passed before me, shrieks and cries blistered my eardrums*, and immediately I knew I was in the right place. A man sat opposite us and watched the group intensely. His hand stretched onto the table and gripped his glass. He looked separate but there was a desire to be part of the group that was clearly evident. At the next tune, he squeezed into the gathering and reached into his pocket. He started rattling a pair of battered spoons in time, clicking the high tempo off his thigh. Turning his head, he looked at us, then laughed and shouted, but I could not make out his words. The music drowned them out. His face was red, weathered and worn by drink and wind, and his mouth was raw with yellowing teeth. The animated man on the Tayto packet looked at me also. He'd taken on the same features. But I could see his words, they were printed out in bold text beside a graphic figure of a man dropping something into a bin. They read 'Keep Ireland Beautiful'.

It was the next morning and I was having breakfast in the dining room at Temple House. The sun was rising and it lit the window to my left with a blinding glow. I peeled the rind from the black pudding on my plate and let the warmth seep into my bones. Walking down to the boathouse, the grass was sodden underfoot. There was water everywhere, as if the world itself was flooded. I loaded the boat and rowed out across the spiky crop of the dead reed bed. This spread out from the shore for a good sixty yards. Just as I thought I'd reached the deeper water another set would appear. Finally, the glinting tops of the broken reeds vanished and the water fell away. The sun had risen fully. I started the engine and put the boat up towards the deep water at the southern end of the lake. I'd known that the water was big but I didn't realise its extent until I was out on it. On the east side the land rose sharply and was crowned with clumps of trees, their branches condensed and sharpened like an anvil by the westerlies that battered Sligo for most of the year. On the west bank it was hard to tell where the land ended and the lake began. The reed beds were 100 yards deep at least and beyond them were the drowned figures of bankside trees, the trunks submerged and the higher branches reached out of the water above them.

The boat passed a group of three small outcrops which were marked on the map I had in my pocket – except here I could really only make out one, half a tree protruding from the water, and beyond it a pole with a ragged flag set in the wind. This was a marker set on the highest ground of the third outcrop. I nearly missed it, it was so faint and isolated. I drove up beyond them and past the island, slowed down and brought the boat back in a loop. The wind was up here; it was only a fresh breeze but once the motor was silent it slapped the waves against the underside of the boat. I slid the anchor over the side and the rope span off from its hole under the prow. It couldn't find the floor of the lake, so I pulled it up and rowed closer into the shore until I felt confident that it would. I took a dead mackerel out of the bucket and with a knife cut through the fish, its spine breaking quietly. I mounted a head on one rig and a tail on the other, adding some swan shot to the top of the trace to take the baits down. The sun was well up by now and the warmth spread through me. The rays caught the waves and crystals of light danced in the reflections on my hands. I sat in the wooden boat, watching the lines from tips of the rod for any sign of movement.

After an hour the rhythm of the slapping waves on the boat and the benevolence of the winter sun were lulling me to sleep. My eyes flickered and I woke with a start. The midday sun cut down through the surface of the lake but could not penetrate it. The boat felt suddenly very small, like a raft of driftwood. A strange mounting nervousness stirred in my belly. A reversal of vertigo. Usually my lines would lie in a shallow arc but here they fell away almost vertically from the rods into the brown peaty water. I knew there were giants right under my feet but they seemed so far down and out of reach. I lifted my baits, pulled the anchor from the grasp of the mud, started the engine, and set off back down the lake. At the northern end, past the boathouse, the lake narrowed into a tight lane, which ran under a stone bridge. Here the water was much shallower, ten feet at the most.

I killed the motor, tipped up the engine and drifted onto

the reed tops. As the boat stilled I dropped anchors off both ends to stop it fast and prevent any drifting. I took a fresh mackerel from the bag, halved it and anointed it with some oil. I cast one bait along the front of the reeds and the other out into the middle of the channel. The afternoon light started to soften. Every now and again wild fowl would scatter from the sanctuary of the trees opposite me. They'd circle a few times and settle. It was a mesmerising pattern.

Suddenly, the line on my right-hand rod was pulled out of its clip. My hand hovered over the butt of the rod. The line in the water started to move off and then stopped. I picked up the rod, turned over the bail arm, turned the handle of the reel to tighten down, and struck. The rod kicked violently and then the handle on the reel span out of my fingers, clipping my knuckles as the fish ran for the first time. It was a good forty yards from the boat before I turned it. It then ran back towards me and it was as much as I could do to keep pace and gather the line before it slackened. It did this two or three times and on each occasion that it ran back out, I could feel the line cutting through the cabbage leaves that grew under the surface. One or two popped up to the surface like random markers. On the fourth run back to the boat I tried to get its head up and have a look at the fish. I could make out a vague shape and then it shot towards the boat and under the boards. The rod smacked down on the rail at the side and the top of the rod plunged down into the water. It was trying to reach the ropes. It was about sheer brute force now; any thought of playing the pike had gone and we slugged it out, the fish diving again and again and me hauling it away from the ends of the boat. I had cramp in my right hand and had to tuck the butt under my arm whilst I pumped some blood back into my fingers. I could feel the fish tiring too. With my left hand I hoisted the landing net over the side of the boat and rested it in readiness. The fish came up. It was huge. The size of a leg with a tail like a head of a spade. It lolled on the surface, thrashing once, angrily, its jaws clamped round the trace. I rolled it over the net, into which it would barely go, clicked off the bail arm, dropped the rod and grabbed the folds of the net with both hands.

I shook. I could barely lift it into the boat. I pulled back the mesh. The fish lay still and beaten. But its jaws were still clamped shut. Its lower one was a mass of bone and muscle, the size of a booted foot, dwarfing my hand as I slid my fingers in under the gill cover. Normally, I could open a pike's mouth with ease like this, the roof staying on the deck and the lower jaw cocking open. I applied some force but it just served to lift the whole head. I tried again and the mouth slit open by a couple of inches. The hooks were at the back of the throat and I had them out in no time. In the roof of the pike's mouth, tucked in between rows of fine razored bone, was another small, size twelve hook. I nicked this and took my hand out from under its gill. I was worried that at any moment the fish was going to go berserk and shred my hands to bits. I slipped it into a sack and placed it back into the water. Reaching for my scales I lifted the sack back up, let the water drain off and hung it onto the hook. The needle span round, through the green and into the orange. It settled, flickering, at twenty-four pounds.

I lowered the fish back into the water and teased the sack off its head. I cupped my right hand around its tail. Instead of lying under the surface the pike lowered its head until it was almost vertical and then opened up its gills. They glowed like halos. I had been mistaken, they were not the wings of a rook, but the wings of an angel. I reluctantly loosened my hold on the tail, the grand pike kicked gracefully, and was gone. I looked out across the water, the sunlight splitting from behind the clouds that were closing in from the south. I was anchored at both ends, and the silvery blue of the surface ran for miles. There were no faces, or voices. The wind had dropped and the quiet was not broken by a single shriek or cry. I sat upright in the boat, my face to the light, and could hear a heart beating in my chest. It was not my own, and the beat was irregular as if fuelled by only one lung. Had I found him, at last, here?

I watched the sun set behind the trees and lifted my baits for the last time. To the south a shower of rain masked half of the sky and the breeze rose again. I raised the anchors, lowered the engine into the water and tried to start it. In the damp and cold of the day the contacts had grown sluggish and feeding too much petrol in I managed to flood it. I lifted it again and slid the oars over the side. The darkness was falling swiftly but I could make out the boathouse. I rowed towards it, the sound of the blades in the water ushering in the end of the day.

As I approached the bank I could make out a figure walking down from the house. In front, running in zigzags across the grass, was a small white dog. I grabbed the blue rope and guided the boat in under the roof, every sound magnified by the water and the walls. A voice from outside asked me if I needed a hand. He introduced himself as Paul, a relative of the owners, who'd recently moved to Sligo from abroad. We chatted and talked about the day whilst I cleaned up the boat and packed away my tackle. Helping me carry things, he walked with me back up towards the house and waved me off at the door, as he lived in another part of the grounds. Inside the hall there was a cool stillness. The room was lit by one light, high above, which cast a sombre glow into all but the corners. On the walls a mounted pike of thirty-three pounds dominated the room. An ancestor of the one I'd caught that afternoon. To one side was an old wooden and glass apothecary's case, its drawers and shelves full of bones and shells. There were other cases, too – stuffed birds, a decaying perch and on the mantelpiece the skull of an old, old pike, its teeth as mint as if they'd been milked that morning. In the middle was a large, oak table and on it two or three huge leather volumes, maps of old Sligo and the house's game book. The floor was tiled in a classic Victorian pattern of red, yellow, blue and white tiles. The whole room seemed inspired by the vacant tenants of the old castle, the Knights Templar themselves, a reliquary, a resting place for many grails and secrets.

I left the room and went to see Deborah. I crossed another hallway with stairs winding up the wall to a higher landing above which was a vast atrium. Doors led off at ground level on all sides and portraits hung from around the walls. I found Deborah in one of the rooms, standing by the fire. There was a look on her face that I was unaccustomed to. Normally, I could return hours late and she would be unflustered, barely inquisitive as to whether I'd caught or not, but now she seemed alarmed.

'I wondered what had happened to you.'

'Why?'

'It's been dark for ages; I just had a feeling that something had happened on the lake, that maybe you'd been drowned.'

As the evening wore on this feeling increased even though I was back in the house. It seemed to grow in retrospect. Something had happened out on the lake at Temple House; I knew that I had been immersed in the water somehow, but on this night it felt more like a baptism than a death.

The next morning when I pulled back the shutters the world was white. A heavy frost had fallen overnight and drawn a dense fog from the ground. Deborah and I walked out into it, but instead of turning right to go down to the lake we turned up the driveway, past the old farm buildings, where dogs barked at us, and down a track that led to a walled garden. Puddles of water on the path were frozen over, the ice breaking underfoot but the sound muffled by the moisture in the air. The walls to the garden were tall, at least fifteen, maybe even twenty feet high. On one side a pair of old doors hung in an archway. Opening one of the doors, we crept inside. A vision lay before us. The space was at least an acre, perhaps even two. On one side was a small orchard, the gnarled branches of the trees covered in a mass of lichen, forming microscopic shapes, forests of holy green trumpets and storm waves frozen onto the bark. There was nothing growing here but there was an overwhelming sense of dormant will. Life was suspended, bludgeoned into the unforgiving ground. It was as if it was a room in a part of the house that was sealed off, its furniture in shrouds, clock and picture shadows on the walls and its shutters closed; the echoes of conversation long since faded and gone, the air still and stale. In the centre of the garden were rows of beds, blocks of Victorian order, their blank earth standing out in the silver grass. In one of them the sets of onions had folded into themselves, in another bed dozens of artichoke crowns stood, their brown stalks blasted black by the cold. Around them all of the trees had given up their fruit, all of the plants had been stripped of their harvest. Above one of the walls a faint glow appeared. It came from above the lake, a slight promise of life falling on the forgotten occupants of a glorious winter garden.

Chapter Ten

'No. No. No. Please, God, no,' young Tom said.
Eddy lunged down into the water with the gaff and
then went overboard to try to get the gaff into the
fish if he could reach him.

It was no good. The great fish hung there in the
depth of water where he was like a huge dark purple
bird and then settled slowly. They all watched him
go down, getting smaller and smaller until he was
out of sight.

'Bimini', from *Islands in the Stream*, Ernest Hemingway

The date is 1937, and a passenger ship cuts through the
steely-blue, white-crested waves towards the opening of
the harbour. Either side of the hull small black shapes race
across the top of the water in a flash and are gone. They are
tiny flying fish, fleeting good spirits for ships in sight of land
and far out at sea. The smell of saltwater changes on the wind
to the dense, choking sense of land, of people living on top of
one another, sweating it out amongst the dust-clad, dark
neighbourhoods that run away back into the city, away from

the docks. On the skyline the silhouettes of cranes and chimneys sit like gangs of metal birds and broken trees, waiting to pick the hold clean and incinerate the waste of a week's voyage.

As the captain steers his boat into the mouth of the harbour, a horn blares and several figures wave from the railings on the shore. The ship is dwarfed by giant black tankers, the rust of weeks at sea clinging to the sheer wall of steel that rises up and up until it cuts out the sun and puts the deck of the ship in a dark shadow. It is so close it takes the breath away, rivets as big as fists, the letters of her name as tall as a man and the anchor chain twisting into the sea, as strong and sure as if it was welded to the seat of the earth. The scent of water is suddenly lost, as is the smell of the streets, the air now thick with the stench of oil and grease, a deep rich vapour, tarry and black, all-pervading, like incense seeping from a holy can. A boy stands staring up at the hulk of the tanker, his lungs filling with the richness of the smell. He is dressed in an airtex shirt, trousers and sandals. His hair is combed across in the sharpest of partings and in the shade you can make out the freckles on his skin. His face is alive and excited, fixed in a look of awe, open mouthed and full of learning, drinking in another sight on this voyage with his father, here at the first stop after Kingston, Jamaica – the harbour in the city of Havana, Cuba. Next to him stands a small suitcase, made of leather, but painted green, on which is an assortment of labels, one written in his father's hand, the blue ink on the label spelling out the boy's name, Kevin Edward Patrick Andrews. A palm of a large hand rests on the top of his head. He can feel the pulse beating through it, and a voice calls to him, 'Come on, son, it's time to go ashore.'

It is Saturday, 6 January 2001, the feast day of Epiphany, over sixty years since my father docked in Havana. I sit stiff and bleary in my seat and peer out of the cabin window of the aeroplane. Tens of thousands of feet below me I can make out faint lights, random, some distant and some definite, like delicate stars in the sky's reflection at night in the sea. There are no swimmer's arms to scatter them here; they are steady and constant, if ever so faint. I gaze down, looking for them to sketch out the shape of the harbour, to light the shadow of the ships docked in her concrete arms, but there is just a blackness. Ten hours have brought me back over the Atlantic Ocean from London to Havana, across a lifetime, and as we lose altitude I feel sick with excitement at the prospect of stepping out into that magic blanket of lights. Most of the other passengers are holidaymakers, transfers from Paris, Europeans in search of the Buena Vista Social Club, students of Che and packaged couples waiting for the armband and the all-you-can't-eat buffet. I am here on a tourist card, too, fifteen pounds from the embassy office off High Holborn, but I am hiding a mission. In my hand is a book, still unthumbed, *Islands in the Stream* by Hemingway, and I grasp it as if it is a bible. I have not read it yet, but will do so here, in homage to the famous sportsman and in memory of an unknown soldier who, to me, was more of a legend. The edges of the pages have yellowed to brown, the illustration and type on the cover look dated and cheap but it is one of my most treasured possessions. On the inside cover there is a dedication, the words desperate and failing, slipping like blunted hooks pulling free at 200 feet,

'Xmas '91.

To my dad

with all my love

John.'

Deborah and I arrive at last at our hotel in the Parque Central, Havana, after spending an hour in Immigration and another looking for our baggage in the chaos of the airport. It is nearly 1 a.m. as the lift takes us up to our room. In England the dawn will soon be lighting the sky bleakly in the east and I think of the cold winds on the Fen, the darkness of the water on a winter morning and of the fish within. I wonder if their spirits can travel half the world and still exert the same influence over me. Thinking of them here, they seem to be twice as powerful, the flashing scales of a roach shining in my mind as if they were made up by a thousand silver threads, iconic and inviting, like a summons from God himself. Outside our shuttered room the noise of a Saturday night in Havana bounces off the walls of the thin streets, the constant rattle of salsa, and the collective harmonies of 100 singers serenading for dollars. From the floor directly above us, the bass thump of the rooftop disco shakes the light fittings. It is winter in Cuba but the night is hot and humid, and in the half-light of our room I long to sleep. I've been up for twenty hours and my head is ready to burst, but I am here and soon I will fish. I close my eyes and hope to dream of the sons of the Atlantic, the giant marlin, the wahoo, the sailfish, tarpon and barracuda – but they are eclipsed by others I've left behind, messengers from Albion, as the room fills with water and above me swim the pike, the perch and the roach. I awake at three, disorientated, and blink in the gloom. I know I am here in body, but I am not complete, as if part of me has refused to make the journey and is still thousands of miles behind, standing by the spate of an English river in the Sunday morning rain.

It is late afternoon the following day, and Deborah and I are sitting on a wooden bench in the doorway of a house in one of the suburbs of old Havana. The houses are single storey, fronted by arches, their paint faded by decades. The roads are empty of cars, replaced instead by skinny dogs, slumped in the shade or barking in the sun. The light pours in through the open door and falls on the stone floor, polished by centuries of feet and washed by storms when the water runs in. A man sits opposite us, in the dark, rocking backwards and forwards on a traditional rocking chair. We only met ten minutes ago and we're on our first bottle of rum. The bottle stands on a plastic tray and we drink it neat from small glass beakers. His laughter fills the room, echoing off the ceiling, where the plaster has fallen away in chunks, exposing the thin slats of the batons which are nailed to the roof. I want a boat, a pair of rods, multiplier reels loaded with 250 yards of line, sets of lures and a good skipper, one who will take me out to prolific grounds, in search of blue marlin, maybe to hunt for wahoo and barracuda and find redemption in the beautiful ocean. The man cannot stop laughing, shaking his head and is rocking back and forth even faster, 'No, no, it's not possible. Look, it is the winter, the storms come in most days, the marlin has gone. You could follow the stream and find him off the Bahamas, but not in a Cuban boat.' He loads me up with another shot of rum and it eases the sickness I feel, the nauseous despair of running through the night and banging on the door of the church, the devil in pursuit, only to find it locked and the priest gone.

The man used to have a boat, he used to fish, long ago, but he gave it up. He would not tell me why, just waved it off with a laugh and another shot. He could help us, but it was more risky now he no longer drove visitors around – it was simpler to carry the African holy men who flocked to the city on their days of worship. They paid well and the police were suspicious of them in a good way, as if stopping the car would elicit a curse. We have dinner together in a Paladares a few blocks away and discuss the merits of Buccanero over Cristal, eat rice and beans and battered chicken. He takes us back into the city once it is late. The streets are dark, save for the cars looming out of the blackness – '50s Lincolns, Buicks, box-shaped '70s Fiats and anonymous '80s coupés, dodging the pot-holes and pits on the road, their headlamps running across our bleary faces like searchlights.

I would not give up. My father had been too ill to read that last gift – or maybe he'd left it untouched for a reason. I could not remember what had prompted me to buy it, perhaps I knew it would be a compendium of all the days we'd shared and of ones I wish we'd shared but never had; fictional lives mingled with our own, building dreams and saying farewells. Here I was in the middle of another dream, desperately trying to turn the fiction into reality, to conjure some magic far from home and dance on top of the waves. I would find the fish. I had to.

I slept far better that night, not waking until gone nine, the sun creeping in across the bed through the louvre cracks in the shutters. The mornings were almost sedate in Havana, the temperature rising fast with the sun, the fug of the city silencing the buzz of scooters and the roar of Russian trucks stacked with mangoes and passengers who'd forsaken the eternal wait for a bus. Deborah and I walked up the Prado, ignoring the cigar sellers every ten yards, the touts offering us everything from lunch to their sister, and out, round the corner onto the Maleçon. Here, a concrete breakwater curved away from us, Corbusian in its beauty, but sudden in its impact. Waves broke frequently over the top of it and drenched the passing cars or cyclo-taxis. They seemed to be reaching out desperately in an attempt to pull the old buildings that stood fifty yards opposite into the sea. Built at the beginning of the twentieth century, the Maleçon was a waterfront parade in a state beyond decay. It was not just the sea that had eaten away at its plaster and stone but time itself, hollowing out the interiors to ruin and setting the wind to play amongst its many open windows and darkened spaces. You could walk the Maleçon for miles, dodging the waves and watching the divers searching for squid under its benevolent walls. It stretched before you, the towers of Vedado shimmering like a mirage in the distance, a pastiche of Miami, the forbidden city.

We passed the mackerel fishermen, standing barefooted on the lip of the wall in primary-coloured shirts and shorts, in gangs of ten or more, shouting excitedly when they'd found a new shoal. Their rods were fibreglass and paired with fixed-spool reels, the salty line spiralling out from the rod tips into the lively water below. Plastic bags sat at their feet, waiting to be filled with Spanish mackerel and carried back down the narrow dusty streets, with their broken sewers flowing down the gutters and peanut sellers crying out from the shade of doorways. I envied the fishermen. I had flown to Cuba without a rod, or a reel, seeking to hire it all once I was here. The simplest of fishing was to be had here, a fifteen-minute walk from my bed and I wanted to join my new companeros up on the wall. On the pavement behind them were discarded catches, inexplicably tossed into the dirt, their flanks brown, their eyes eerily popped and vacant. I stooped but could not pick one up, as gestures and cries flew in my direction along with shaking heads and stern expressions. They were to be left in the sun, for their skin to shrivel and dry, as if in sacrifice, to secure the rest of the catch. The ease and grace of the fishermen made me smile and lifted my spirits. I was beginning to change my 'had' to 'would'.

As we approached Vedado, the road swung round to the right and in the arc waves crashed over with increasing frequency. The pavement was green with algae and the saltwater ran off after each break, clattering down through the iron grilles of the drain at the side of the road with a rushing sound as if it was falling far, far below. The sun was high above us now, and in the midst of this winter's day I could feel it burning my skin and pushing me back from the sea and into the shade of the streets behind. Up on the hill, past the Rampas with its bucket shops and peso cinemas you suddenly came across peace. The streets widened slightly and avocado trees grew, their roots gleaning moisture from the foundations of the old walls. On one of these, a brass nameplate was nailed, the words 'Museo Napoleonico', glinting amid the leaves. We went through an archway, the cool of a marbled hall and into the garden of an old Spanish colonial villa, with more avocado trees and small birds singing in their branches. Despite this, and more likely because of it, there was, for the first time since we'd arrived, a silence here.

The garden and its villa had belonged to an Italian anarchist who'd bought the relics of the emperor's life at auction and transported them here at the end of the nineteenth century – another obsessive collector, on an unknown odyssey at the end of a previous century. Here, there was a library of books, occupying the fifth floor, encased behind glass and leather, words locked away forever. On a stairway there was a statue of an eagle, set in gold, turned into a lantern, lighting the wall above. There was the rich smell of polished teak, an empty dining table, set in hope for guests, but the shutters were closed in the knowledge that they would never come. There was one of Napoleon's teeth, set in a glass case and the bedspread under which he sweated and died in exile on the island of St Helena, and beside it a pale, cream death mask. I stood over it and looked long at his expression. It was the same as that of any saint you'd find slain in crypts along the routes of the crusaders. Calm, still and beaten. I listened for the ticking of a watch but there was none.

From the roof of the villa you could see out across the whole of the city. Clouds had blown over in the time we'd been inside. It had felt so short, but we'd been there for hours. The colour of the city was a sandy grey and the white-horsed Atlantic to our left threatened to envelop its flat expanse. Up here the Maleçon was much more than thoroughfare or fishing platform; it stood between Havana and extinction. With the clouds came the rush of the wind through the trees below, which would soon be followed by tropical rain. We descended the stairs, the daylight failing and dim, the attendants sitting still and dutiful in their chairs, smiling at us as we went, keepers of teeth, oils and clay, guardians of a fallen emperor.

The rain came in squalls and as we scuttled quickly through the streets of Centro it soon turned the dust to mud and brought the brackish pond under the street to life beneath our feet. People sheltered in their doorways, still shouting across the street, their conversation like song. Baseball games between children carried on uninterrupted by rain – tomorrow's ghetto stars arguing over the makeshift wooden bats held together with a nail, passers-by hollering encouragement and dodging the stone wrapped in tape that made for a ball as it flew towards the boundary of the next block. Steam spilled from pans on peso stalls, tucked into small spaces, their meals painted up in flowery text on the wall. There were empty bars, selling only locally brewed rum, their interiors like Edward Hopper paintings and mahogany L-shaped bars backed by box shelves on which stood plain bottles without labels, plugged with recycled corks. Solitary barmen stood in the corner smoking cigars stolen from the factory opposite the Museo de la Revolucion, waiting for custom – or, in one, shouting advice to his friends as they dismantled a motorbike on the floor of the bar, its wheels in the air and the engine lame and exposed. There were no paintings of Che, or Fidel lookalikes in boots and beards, just life as it had been just before and since the revolution.

We ducked into the lee of a building as a black Chevrolet splashed slowly past us, a panther's head set in chrome on the bonnet, wipers like straws, an upright driver at the wheel and a passenger sitting in the back, partially obscured by tinted glass but his silhouette clearly visible. He had a classic post-war profile, a sharp, short-back-and-sides haircut and a brown towelling T-shirt with open collar. His arm rested on the side of the window frame, tanned and freckled. On it was a Cyma Diving Star wristwatch, newly purchased, its second hand ticking round effortlessly, its four numerals, three, six, nine and twelve, painted in luminous green. Between his fingers the man held a cigarette, untipped and recently lit. It seemed so white in his brown hands. The smoke from it carried out through a thin crack at the top of the window and blew into my face.

The buildings ran away in a V and I watched the black car as it made its way down the street, getting smaller and smaller until, at the end, it turned right into the traffic, in the direction of La Floridita. This was a neon-flagged cocktail bar and restaurant that stood to the north of the Parque Central. It was made famous both in fiction and in real life by Hemingway and was the scene of his lone drinking exploits, where he, along with a bartender, invented the Daiquiri. His record for drinking them stood at thirty in a single day, after which we are led to believe that he walked unaided out into the night. Two long shots of rum, a splash of lime and plenty of ice. As I sat at the bar I peeled the gold paper off the neck of my Cristal lager. Homage was one thing; a hangover before the night was out was another. I looked around me. The interior was lit by lights behind star-shaped shades, the bar protruding out from the back wall in a flattened horseshoe. Along it were stools on one side and bartenders on the other, dressed in white shirts, trousers and cropped red tuxedos. On the floor were sets of tables and chairs, and beyond them a cream banquette which ran the length of the window. The latter was draped in sets of regal curtains. The bartenders mixed and dealt from a red Formica bar-station behind them. Above the cabinets that were set into the bar were the words '*La Cuna del Dalquiri*' – 'The Cradle of the Daiquiri'. These gave the station a serious air, as if it was an impervious piece of history. You felt that if the staff of La Floridita celebrated Christmas they would do so not by building cribs with shepherds and lambs, but with replicas of '*La Cuna*' with miniature bottles of mixer and fake baskets of fruit.

I looked around again. The bar was full, animated conversation and the hum of music coming from one corner. To my left, mounted on the wall, was the bronze bust of Hemingway himself, which looked more like a popular image of Lenin than it did the writer. Perhaps that was a dig at the photograph behind me on the wall, a record of the only time Hemingway had met and spoken to Castro, in 1960, at the Torneo di Hemingway, a marlin fishing competition in which Fidel and Che shared a boat. Neither won but that didn't stop the judges from awarding Fidel a trophy for heaviest weight of marlin 'caught'. In the photo both Ernest and Fidel are smiling as the latter is presented with his honorary trophy. There is no sign of Che; he'd probably slipped away quietly, to the nearest bar for a shot of neat rum, or to fix a motorbike. The following year Hemingway was dead.

I'd hoped to find both my ghosts talking here, over a cocktail and a beer: the writer of *Islands* and the soldier from the car, his cigarette smoke filling the bar and the glass ashtray full of stubs, both talking about their wars and their children. Behind the bar, above the crib, was an old painting. It depicted the old port of Havana as you would have once seen it from the sea. The lighthouse on the rock of Morro stood proud above the bay and at the entrance to the harbour an old sailing ship was making its way gracefully into port. The Malecón was not yet built and classical-looking stone houses stood on the shore. The ship was probably a Spanish galleon, loaded with gold and wine. The painting was in oil, stained by the tar of a million smokes. Its sea was black and the sky was a dark green. It was the opposite of the kind of paintings that the hero of *Islands*, the artist Thomas Hudson, painted. His pictures hung in bars too, but they were bright, suffused with energy and focused usually on one main character, a raging water spout, or a giant sailfish. They were grand, carefree and weightless. At the end of the first story, after a summer of fishing, in which one of the sons, David, has an epic struggle with a huge sailfish of a thousand pounds or more, Hudson receives a telegram. It tells him that two of his sons, including David, have been killed in an accident whilst on the road to Biarritz with their mother. I stared at the painting in La Floridita. If Hudson had painted after that, I wondered if his seas would have been as black, and his skies that dark biblical green. Perhaps there were ghosts in here after all, even if the steady flow of tourists and predictable musical ensemble playing 'Chan Chan' did their best to exorcise them.

The next morning, as I lay in bed, just awake, my eyes hid a dull ache in my head. I opened them slowly and waited for them to focus on my wristwatch. I could hear the second hand ticking, like the marching of boots on a desert road, and although the numerals on the face had long lost their luminosity, I could just make them out. Three, six, nine, twelve. The hands came into view as I tightened my focus on the face. By the letters they obscured on the legend of the watch – the 'C' of 'Cyma' was covered and the 'Diving' had lost its star – I could tell it was five to eight. I pulled a card from my wallet and reaching for the telephone dialled 24-68-48, the number of the Marina Hemingway. A woman answered and I asked if the fishing boats would be going out that morning. 'No, no, it is too rough, the low pressure is very deep, the storm will be big.' I could have finished the sentence for her, '. . . it is winter, the storms come in most days, the marlin has gone.'

I thanked her and replaced the receiver. My head dropped back onto the pillow, I closed my eyes and swore at the morning. I had had enough of being led through the streets of Havana by ghosts, imagined and real. I wanted to be out on the sea, with my baits at 200 feet, reading my dedication for real, waiting for a clear response. Was that what I meant when I said I would not give up? It must have been.

Chapter Eleven

Lose (looz), v.t. & i (*lost* pr. law or lo-; *-able*). Be deprived of, cease to have, let or have pass from one's control or reach or power of finding (*l.* one's *life*, one's *father*, *consciousness*).

The Pocket Oxford Dictionary of Current English, 1924

We took the bus south out of Havana towards the sixteenth-century town of Trinidad. The journey should have taken about five hours but was longer, as the driver took several detours to deliver food and rum to friends in outlying villages along the way. We also stopped at a services in a tent by the side of the road. Here, amid the flies, two men served us ham and cheese sandwiches drowned in bad ketchup and raw mustard. We washed them down with the only liquid it was fast becoming safe to drink in Cuba: cold lager. We had these at the side of the six-lane freeway, Cuba's busiest road, and waited. Waited for traffic to pass. After five minutes a truck loaded with sugar cane limped past us in a cloud of diesel fumes. Our driver then called us back onto the bus. We were still only halfway to Trinidad. Our destination was not in the direction from which the sugar-cane lorry had come. It lay in the other, from which there was no traffic at all.

It started to grow dark as we approached Trinidad, the bus dwarfed by the giant looming presence of the mountains of the Sierra Del Escambray. It was still just light but the dusk was so intense it was claustrophobic. Slowly, a phosphorescent but muted glow filled the cabin of the bus. Through the windows on the right of the bus spilled a vision. The seas off the south of Cuba. They were so completely different in appearance and character to the Atlantic off Havana. The water was calm but for a gentle ripple and was a pale-green colour. It lapped up onto the shore, which was littered with empty crab shells and sticks of weed. In places the sand had washed across the road, and here it was difficult to tell where the road ended and the sea began. We passed a wooden jetty with a few boats tied up against the side. They beckoned. But I knew that taking one would mean rowing forever towards the horizon, waking dehydrated, out of your head with sunstroke, fearful of attacks by sharks; drifting over the Cayman Trench, not yet in sight of Jamaica.

———

It is late one January evening, 1990, and a man walks south across Hungerford Bridge. It has stopped raining hard, and the sky is quickly clearing, the pink glow of the city reflecting off the river and giving life to every shadow. As he digs his hands deeper into his pockets, one of them touches something that has fallen into the lining of the coat. It is a scrap of paper. On it are the words 'Hunt for Britain's rarest fish'. The words stick in his head and then he remembers.

Surely, he'd posted that off years ago? It was for his son. Maybe he'd been distracted when the tea trolley came round. It was his favourite part of the day – a laugh and a joke with the tea lady, a rare piece of camaraderie these days. The tea was stewed, as always, and served in a green HMSO-issue cup and saucer. It was this that made it taste so bad. Still, with a biscuit it was passable. He remembered when he had to make tea from water in the jungle of Borneo, using the rain that had gathered in the giant leaves of the lower canopy and tilting them down so that it poured into a billy-can; crouched in the dead banana leaves with leeches on your legs, humidity that made even your eyeballs sweat – that tea was the drink of the gods.

In the distance a huge, flat-bedded barge steamed under a bridge, heading towards him. The wind had caught the canvas and ripped it open exposing the containers inside it. In the reflected light the man could make out the blue-and-yellow symbol on the sides. It read 'Fyffes – The Blue Label Brand'. That was another thing he missed – decent bananas, like the small ones he used to eat in Jamaica. He had stopped walking now and was leaning against the railings at the side of the bridge. He watched as the barge sailed down the river towards him. Within seconds it was under his feet and gone. The man stood there for what seemed like a very long time. In the cold he could feel an ache deep inside his chest. That was the problem with too much stewed tea and biscuits, these days they seemed to give him bad indigestion and heartburn.

When we reached Trinidad it was completely dark. Stepping off the bus we were confronted by a line of people standing by the gates holding up signs and mispronouncing names. It was as if the entire town had turned up to see the arrival of the visitors. I approached the boy who was calling out my surname and shook him by the hand. He introduced me to his father and they led Deborah and me away and up the street. It was cobbled and sloped into a V, with a drain running down the centre. On either side were single-storey houses with flat tiled roofs and tiny doorways. The smell was not that of any city or town I had ever been to. The air was so clear that you could be forgiven for thinking that you were high up in the mountains rather than at sea level, but its taste was primitive, ancient, like something from the Bible. Individual shouts called out from adjacent streets and you could hear snatches of conversation as you passed people's windows. Even though it was cold for Cuba, everybody's door, without exception, stood open. We stumbled through the narrow streets, our feet slipping on the large cobbles. It felt distinctly as though we had arrived in an old settlement, one that sat beyond the other side of the world, somewhere between sunset and sunrise.

After dropping off our bags we went for a walk. The streets spread out like spokes from the centre of the town, and as they did so they rose steeply. If you carried on they would turn to dirt and lead you off into the Sierra. The conversations of earlier had died down now, and there was an eerie silence as we explored the small town. At the top of one of the streets was the Plaza Mayor. This was a tiny square of tight cobbles within which was a garden planted with miniature palm trees and garishly painted plaster icons. Dominating the small space was the imposing Iglesia de la Santisima Trinidad, a huge nineteenth-century sandstone church, its steps and pillars creating a façade that would not have looked out of place on a private chapel in the gardens of a Victorian estate. Its doors were locked. Above them shone a dim light, its beam throwing grotesque shadows off the occupants of the garden and onto the walls opposite, creating its own cinema of shadows. Here in the heartlands of the revolution the impossible had happened. On the white plaster stood a giant figure of Mary set against the spikes of a palm – a mimic of the Statue of Liberty, stripped of her torch, her skirts trimmed and her hands joined in prayer.

The Peninsula de Ancon lies about five kilometres to the south of Trinidad. At 8 a.m. the following morning, after a night of fitful sleep, broken by fighting dogs and the centuries-old cry of the bread man doing his rounds on foot at 6 a.m., I stood in the office of its small marina. Two men, who looked as though they'd had less sleep than me between them, were smoking and arguing as to which boat could take us out. I drew my crude sketch of a barracuda. They broke off from their argument, nodded at me, and then carried on. Then one walked out and the other said, 'Okay, 200 dollar. You feesh.' I handed over the cash, which he pocketed. There was an awkward silence. It was the first time since we'd arrived that I had done something, like booking a bus ticket, or arranging to stay in someone's house, where I hadn't been asked to produce my passport. I felt elated. We really had made it to the other side of the world, even if they did still deal in dollars. The man then ushered Deborah and me across some scrub and onto a wooden pontoon. At the back of this was a bar containing a rusty fridge and a giant plastic inflatable bottle of Cristal. Next to it stood a bartender. He spoke a little English and explained that the boat was coming to pick us up here at 9 a.m. The 200 dollars included as much rum, Coke and cervesas as we could drink, but no water – for that there would be a charge of one dollar a bottle. Whilst we were waiting, he asked, why didn't we have a Mojito? When I shook my head he laughed, and said, 'Germans. Always lager.'

The pontoon stood on a shallow inlet which seemed to be made up more of salt than of water. Fluorescent green in colour, it was broken up by small islands on which dense scrub grew. From around the back of one of these our boat appeared. You could not guess her age from her appearance, but I'd say she was about twenty to thirty years old. The engine spat out grey diesel fumes as the boat pulled up next to the pontoon. From bow to stern she was about twenty-five feet in length, blue and white in colour, and built completely from wood, with a low-slung cabin and open back. There was no flying bridge, no chair to be strapped into if you connected with a giant tuna or sierra. The boat carried no flag and looked completely anonymous. The skipper emerged from behind the salt-covered cabin windscreen dressed in jeans and a yellow vest. The vest advertised a car-hire agency in Miami. His mate wore jeans and a straight white T-shirt without a logo. Both were without shoes. The idling engine coughed and we jumped on board. The bartender shouted after us and threw down a slab of Cristal and the inevitable bottles of Havana Club. These were stowed in a dustbin of ice away from the sun. The skipper turned the boat, and, with the mountains in the background, pushed us out through the narrow channels between the small cays that led from the marina and out into the open sea. Above the wheel was a set of instruments. Wires were chased around the frame of the windscreen and were taped to holes in the wood. They then disappeared. Above the dials and screens, directly over the skipper's head, there were two small rectangular black boxes. One of these was a navigational aid and the other was an echo sounder. Our course was set at

21 degrees 41. 442 North

79 degrees 55. 668 West

Course 133.3

Speed 13.6 Kt.

The screen on the echo sounder was blank. Here the water was still shallow; we were heading out to where it dropped off to 200 feet.

At the back of the boat José, the mate, was putting up the rods. These stood at either side of the boat in sockets that swallowed about a foot and a half of the butts. The rods were set at forty-five degrees. They were about six or seven feet long, fibreglass, and manufactured in the '70s by Penn. Their fittings and eyes looked as if they had been replaced several times. The reels were large brass multipliers – Penn Internationals. The line of about fifty pounds breaking-strain sat on a drum that ran inside the open face of the reel. Tied to the end of the line was a steel wire trace, on the end of which was a large wooden lure, about the size of a big cigar, but painted naively to look like a small fish. Off this hung two sets of rusty, barbed treble hooks. A plastic vane was glued into the mouth of the lure, again at forty-five degrees, to make it dive deep in the water.

The boat ploughed on. The shoreline was growing flatter and flatter as the engine opened up and the shallow hull started to beat down on top of the waves that grew larger the further out we went. We passed huge iron buoys, their paint peeling, bleached white by the guano from the bird shit, rocking gently in the swell, marking reefs and sandbanks. Their frames were like the gutted structures of abandoned buildings. Beyond them there was nothing but the open sea.

We left the last of the buoys behind us and the skipper shouted at José. Other than tackling up the rods he had done nothing more than smoke and stare out from the back of the boat at the diminishing land. They talked and remonstrated, shrugging shoulders and pointing to the horizon. To our left lay the mottled grey of a mackerel sky and beneath this the slender line of a cay which seemed to detach itself from the sea in the heat haze. You could just make out the green trees that grew out of its sand. The skipper slowed the engines and José tapped me on the shoulder and pointed at the rods. Flicking the brake off the drum of one of the reels, he paid out eighty yards of line into the smooth water behind the boat. I did the same with the other rod and then stood it in the socket. I sat on the edge of the boat behind one of the rods. The lines from both ran out in an arc from the rod tips, the lures running through the wake, occasionally breaking the surface of the water. When this happened José would tug on the line and force them back under the surface. The sun lit up the sea like crystal. From the pit of my stomach an intense feeling of relief and joy spread through me until I smiled involuntarily. I had found a boat, a pair of rods, multiplier reels loaded with line, sets of lures and a good skipper. My head filled with the sound of the engine gunning and the splash of the waves as we hit them. Deborah was sitting up on the bench that ran round the inside of the cabin, in her denim jacket, my dad's old bush hat and her Superga's. This was happiness. José caught my smile and acknowledged it with one in return. He slapped me on the shoulder and said, 'Si, barracuda,' before stepping behind and reaching into the ice for our first Cristal of the day.

Before he made it to the cabin one of the drums on the reels began to race and the rod slammed round into a curve. José shouted to the skipper, who stalled the boat in a wash of surf, and I grabbed the rod, pulling the butt into my pelvis, and stemmed the run by holding the rod with my left hand and tightening the drag on the reel with my right. I could feel the thump, thump, thump of a hooked fish. The previous arc of the line had given way to a tautness that shot off at an acute angle into the water. Suddenly, slackness. José yelled at me and I reeled frantically with my right hand. The fish was heading back to the boat. I caught up with it and the line went tight once again. Then it ran once more. I felt the shake of its body before the reel buzzed and the line paid out fast. Before I could halt it I felt the loose bowing of the line and knew it was off. I shook my head and indicated to José that it had gone. He smiled again and said, 'Si, si, barracuda.'

The whole episode had taken less than a minute. Adrenalin had now mixed with my earlier joy. My eyes were like plates and my heart tight. I reeled the lure in and on its balsa back you could see the chunks that the fish's teeth had taken out of it. José checked the leader and paid the line out again. In the water beneath you could make out the dark mass of a reef. Over these reefs the lone barracuda hunted, feeding on the small fish, known locally as *Sardino* and occasionally gorging its own.

The barracuda is known to grow to a weight of 100 pounds. It was christened *Syhyraena Barracuda* in 1792 by a naturalist called Walbaum. The body takes the form of a bullet. Its head is the shape of an arrow. The mouth is a black tunnel of razor-wire teeth and the jaw is lined with protruding molars that twist in different directions to puncture the flesh of prey. Their flanks are silver with vertical black bars which fade quickly – and black blotches which strangely intensify – after death. There are streamlined fins either side of its tight gills and a small spined dorsal that sits proud on top of its back. Its anal fins are shaped like sharply cut sails. The tail is twice the width of the fish and is the only part of the body that looks out of character. Triangular in shape, it has an almost oriental pattern cut into it. Seen in profile, this has the same outline as that of a golden eagle in flight. Until they're a weight of fifteen pounds the barracuda live in shoals, known as schools; hundreds of fish synchronised in a wall of silver. Once over fifteen pounds the fish become solitary, marauding around the edges of the reef and sulking in the deep waters beyond it. The barracuda thrives in warm seas the breadth of the world over. You'll find it first in the waters along the Tropic of Capricorn and its distribution is intense just north and south of the equator. North of the Tropic of Cancer it slowly dies out and once you reach the latitudes off the coast of

Portugal in the Atlantic it is as good as extinct. It resembles only one other fish on the whole planet. A fish that lives in cold freshwater far to the north, one that was christened long before it. The *Esox Lucius*. Pike.

José lit another cigarette, tugged once more on the lines, and the lures skipped off the surface before being dragged back under once more. The sun was right above us. It was noon and the water shone like a furnace. It was hard to imagine that it was cold to the touch. I attempted to ask if the light would push the fish down but José shrugged and pointed to a spot off the back of the boat. Small mackerel jumped from the waves about ten feet behind our baits and then, in a flash of surf, a barracuda attacked. The reel sang again. I pulled the rod up and hit the fish back. The top half bent into a solid curve and then about 50 yards in front of me the fish came out of the water in an instant explosion. This fish felt smaller than the last but it raced over the reef from right to left with more speed, before jumping again. Each time it did so the line slackened off for a moment before the clutch turned over and its sound told me I was still connected. After its short fight the fish was beaten and I pumped it up to the back of the boat. José reached down, grasped the line and swung the fish over onto our feet. Out of the water, against the white paint of the wooden deck, it was as if it had fallen from the sky, an angel without a parachute. José pulled the hooks from its mouth and hit it twice with a wooden club that lay at the back of the boat. The fish twitched, its fins shivering, and expired. The bars on its back grew paler whilst the black spots seemed to appear beneath them, like tiny broken windows. Pulling open the lid of the hold, José slid the fish quickly into the cool and shut the hatch with a bang. I felt a sudden deep pang of sadness at how swiftly the life of a beautiful fish had ended, as every so-called hunter must do – an empty victor, the remaining survivor.

Over the next hour, with the sun still high above us, we caught two or three more. Then the skipper asked José to take the wheel whilst he opened the hatch and pulled out one of the fish. He then hopped over the back of the boat onto the boards where he knelt down and proceeded to clean and gut the fish in the sea. He worked quickly with the knife, slicing open its stomach and tearing out the insides in one swift movement. They fell into the churning foam followed by a shower of scales, scraped from the sides. There was a small gas stove in the front of the cabin, a 'Hillerange by Seaward'. On it was a blackened frying pan and next to it an old plastic bottle half filled with oil. Its label was bleached by the sun that shone in through the window each day. Within seconds the smell of frying fish steaks filled the boat. As it did so the sunshine receded, the years vanished, the miles shrank and I was back in a small cottage on the Isle of Skye . . . It is the summer of 1977. The ceiling is low and the walls are whitewashed. A small lamp lights the room. It stands on a table which is covered by a map and a can of pale ale. A man sits over the map talking to his wife through the door of the kitchen. Their son sits in the corner listening to them. The scene draws a line under the end of the day. It closes the door on the outside world and its threats. The room is a cocoon of security, its threads wound by thousands of evenings spent in the same way – the three of them round the table, eating and talking about nothing in particular. There is the smell. The smell is always the same, the clinging veil of cooking oil, spent matches, cigarette and pipe smoke. The smell of home.

My reverie is broken by the skipper handing me a plate and a can of Cristal. Deborah and I share the white flaky flesh of the barracuda. It's the first decent meal we've had for four days, and this, combined with its echoes of my childhood, makes it seem like a divine gift. Never have I appreciated a meal so much. I offer the plate to José and the skipper but they refuse. José in particular seems shocked and unimpressed that we could eat the barracuda, dismissing it with a wave of the hand and a shake of the head. Deborah and I laugh to ourselves and feast, like ravenous birds. In our laughter we do not know that the barracuda carries a poison, christened 'cigatuera'. It originates from venomous algae on the reef, which are food for the smaller reef fish that in turn the barracuda gorge themselves on. A single dose can kill a dog and cripple a man.

I am halfway through the plateful, when the Penn starts to scream and the rod is pulled round viciously so that it is almost horizontal. I grab it and try to pull it up vertically. The reel is still screaming, its line stripping off faster than an anchor rope falling into infinity. There is a force on the other end that I have never felt before. If this is a barracuda, then it is one that is longer than six feet and heavier than twelve stones. This, I know, is impossible, for that would make it in the region of 200 pounds. The skipper stalls the boat and for the first time you can really feel the rock of the open water. Five hundred yards to our left is a small cay, its bushes and trees hemmed in by a thin patch of sand. It is barely a couple of acres in size. Either side of it, waves break over its reef.

The fish is heading across in this direction. All I am aware of is the immense physical presence to which I am tied, as if an electrical current is running between the fish, the line, the rod and my hands. Every split second gives me the sense that I am about to lose control. The flight of the fish is on the verge of being untouchable. José reels the other line in frantically. The skipper is standing next to me. It is the first time he has looked animated. I clasp the rod with both hands. The line is still paying out. The skipper looks at me and then flicks up the clutch to slow the line down. It has three settings: free, strike and full. The first gives no resistance, the second strong resistance and the third none. The brass lever stops between strike and full. I wait for the fish to turn. I stop breathing. Everything tightens up, the line sings, the rod is wrenched down again, and then there is a crack like a pistol shot. The rod straightens and my feet hit the floor of the boat again.

There is a rush of activity. On my rod, the remaining line is checked, a new trace is tied on and a large rubber artificial squid attached to its swivel. The lure on the other is swapped for a larger version, its hooks the size of a small hand. The lines are paid out into the turquoise sea. The skipper turns to me, shrugs, shakes his head and gives me a resigned look. We cannot understand each other through speech, which is just as well as our expressions probably unwittingly blame each other for the loss. 'Sierra,' says the skipper, 'grande, grande.'

There was now a raised sense of expectation. The small barracuda that had been coming to the boat had been replaced by the phantom of the reefs, a giant Spanish

mackerel, known as the *Sierra O Serrucho*. It was said to grow
to a maximum weight of thirty pounds. It was one of these
that had snapped my line of fifty. The skipper was convinced.

We did not have to wait long for another take, the now
familiar sound of the reel screeching above the low drone of the
engine, hailing another fish. The water beneath our feet fell to
over 200 feet and within its draught this one ran like hell. It
lacked the power of the sierra but it had double the speed. I
checked the runs lightly, letting the line pay out freely. Once
each one had stopped I cranked the fish towards the boat. It
came in quickly, each time, before setting off again. Its runs got
shorter and shorter until it was right underneath us but still
out of sight, far below in the blue deep. I was determined to
win this time. My shoulders and my gut hauled it up and
within forty feet of the surface I saw it shimmer. A wonderful
silvery-blue flash in the water. A gorgeous apparition that
cleansed my mind of loss at once. A flicker of redemption.

The skipper coached me in Spanish but my ears were shut
to it. He jumped onto the boards at the stern of the boat, gaff
in hand, and implored me to take it easy. The fish came up
with ease. And there it lay on the surface, a barracuda of
around twenty-five pounds, strong, indignant and glorious.
It was as if it was newly born from the belly of a sea monster.
I waited for it to sprout wings and continue its resurrection.
In one movement it told me clearly that it belonged down
there, amongst the cities of coral and plains of sand that
wrapped themselves around the world like a crown. Lifting
its head from the water its jaws opened and the fish spat the
hooks, erupted in a shower of spent scales and was gone. It
had been within touching distance.

Chapter Twelve

Island (il-), n. Piece of land surrounded by water;
detatched or isolated thing.

The Pocket Oxford Dictionary of Current English, 1924

The hunt had now been raised to a new level. I had come so
close to turning fiction into reality in Trinidad that I was
gripped by a fervour I had not known before. I did not care
what I had been told about the Atlantic in the winter; instead
I felt a compulsion to return to Havana and take the first cab to
the Marina Hemingway. I wanted to step into the pages of the
book I had given Dad that last Christmas. My outrageous belief
– that if that was possible then so might be the dream that I
would find my father amidst its story – was growing stronger
by the hour. Suddenly, the ghosts of earlier in the week had
become shockingly real.

To get to the Marina from Havana my short journey took me
through an American fairytale, the suburb of Miramar.
Wherever you pick your cab up in the city the environment is
much the same: the grimy, doleful streets, their throng of
people getting by to the constant thud and treble-splitting

whine of salsa, played at a point beyond full volume on radios that are more common than bread. Row after row of buildings on the verge of collapse. An occasional wooden wheelbarrow of lettuce or beet. The taxi driver pulls out into traffic and the smell of the sewer is freshened by the breeze through the window. He drives up to the Malecón and heads west out of the city. There is a roundabout surrounded on four sides by metal billboards, freshly painted, heralding another year of revolutionary struggle, the forty-second. A burning cigar, the hat and the beard, a raised sub-machine gun. A declaration of a victory designed to give purpose to all the greyness of existence here: the twenty-four hour shifts in the hospitals; the public-sector pay, if you are lucky to be at the top of your profession, of twenty-six dollars a month; the bread queues; the black-market meat; the fish ban; the youth camps; the restrictions upon travel. This is one of the last and longest surviving Communist countries in the world, where equality is still an ideal. And then, almost immediately, I am aware of a different smell coming through the window of the taxi. It is that of freshly mown grass. The cab is cruising down a road free of potholes. To each side are kerbstones and trimmed lawns that belong to exquisite '30s villas. There are trees and sprinklers, pink stucco, cars and swimming pools. You could be forgiven for calling the road a boulevard. In Miami this place would not have stood out perhaps, another set of condos built on stolen lives. In Cuba this place is astonishing, a pocket of the island that has been preserved since 1958, kept in pristine order, a confusing monument to imperialism, an orchard of temptation.

The cab was waved through at the gate and we drove up past

the canals and artificial waterways. At the end of the tarmacked road was another monument, our hotel, this time built in homage to Russia, a distinctly '70s-style eastern-bloc monolith. It was *Hotel El Viejo El Mar*, or 'The Old Man and the Sea'. A concrete marlin jumped in the waterless fountain outside its doors. The palm trees that had been planted around it, the swimming pool devoid of people, the rows of empty balconies and the communications mast on top of the roof made it feel like the set of an unmade B-movie. Nothing inside altered that sense. The interior was huge by Cuban standards, filled with palms standing against flock wallpaper, a lone pool table with blue baize, and a reception desk. The air was stale, as if it had been imported in a sealed box from the industrial heartland of Eastern Europe. Our room was on the fifth floor. It had two beds, an empty minibar, a bathroom with a broken light, a leaking toilet and an air-conditioning unit that dripped constantly. This was the only sound you could hear. The windows were covered in a thick yellow film of salt and looked out over the deserted grounds. Beyond was the sea. The sun set whilst I was in the shower, and when I came out of the bathroom the ocean seemed a world away.

Stepping out into the humid air outside the hotel was a surprise after a couple of hours inside. There had been an absence of mosquitoes on our trip so far, the dry season depriving them of their breeding grounds. In the Marina, there were seven or eight artificial canals, built to house boats, one or two of which were squared off into pools where water-skiers could perform. These had been warmed all day by the sun, and now, in the evening, you could sense the hatch. The place was deserted. A guard chatted to his mate in the cabin at the head of the road, but as we walked down towards Papa's Bar, we came across no one. The bar was a ten-minute walk from the hotel, past trimmed lawns, the occasional light, skeletal palms and silent yachts. It was a low-level '60s building downlit by lights that shone brightly from underneath the bar top. There was a musty smell and a lone bartender. In one corner was a wooden cabinet containing the Hemingway Trophy, awarded to the winner of the annual Blue Marlin tournament. The box that housed it was made of glass and framed in wood. The silver bodywork on the trophy was degenerating, the months since its last outing eating at its gleam a little more each day. There must have only been a tiny amount of air within the case, a lungful perhaps, and yet if the trophy stayed locked in the box for more than a year, if the tournament was not fished for some reason, it would turn black before the next one.

Deborah and I ate in a deserted room at the top of the spiral staircase that wound up from the back of the bar. On its walls were faded black-and-white prints of the trophy's winners from the '60s and '70s. Tanned draft dodgers with sun-bleached blond manes stood next to four, 500-pound marlin with their names and the weight of the catch chalked up on the flanks of the dead fish. The marlin were tied by their gills to wooden gallows and their tails trailed on the ground. To hoist them completely would have snapped the framework like it was balsa. The men had a distant look – euphoric, in shock, their eyes and faces saddened by the sepia tint. Next to them stood the skipper or mate from their boat, both dressed in cut-off denims and nothing else. They looked like hunters from a colonial age, lost forever.

I had seen pictures like this somewhere before. Amongst the

belongings I claimed after my father's death was an album of his photographs he had taken during his years in India at the end of the war and leading up to partition. The album tells the story of a young man of nineteen exploring a continent on the other side of the world. There are shots of Hindu temples on Mount Abu, dozens of Shivas carved into pillars and vaulted roofs. There are shots of an oasis, its surface like glass, ringed by ghostly palms, and underneath them, in Dad's handwriting, white ink on the black paper, are the words, 'Mt. Abu – Midnight Jan '45'. On other pages you see his journey, his training in Mhow, men pulling jeeps out of rivers, linemen at 'Khana' time. There are pictures of leave in Bombay, swimming pools at the Cricket Club of India, two figures walking away from the camera along the empty curve of Marine Drive, more temples in Bilaspur, and a portrait of his father in New Delhi, August 1945. A lucky coincidence of wartime, their postings crossing. On one page there is a blurred picture of '15 Battalion Para Regiment' at Malir. Twenty, maybe thirty, men are sitting, crouching and standing around their flag, their brown faces and white teeth facing the camera. My father is amongst them, in the next picture in the back of a Dakota, everyone's expressions stern and tense, and then a sequence of four shots, the men in front of Dad falling through space, legs straight, arms beside their bodies, the parachutes just beginning to unfurl in the cloud. Page after page of army life. Comrades, railway lines, billets, men writing letters home. On one, underneath the 'Sacred Crocodiles at Pir Mangho', there are three shots of Dad, sitting in the sand, his boots covered in dust, his khaki combat trousers rolled up in the heat, shirt off and bush hat buttoned up on one side. At his feet is a field radio set and on his face a look of concentration.

Beneath this are his words, 'THE . . . SIGNALS . . . TYPE (Yoke, Victor, Zebra, Nothing heard, RE-NET!!!)'.

We left the bar and walked out into the night. Clouds were crossing the sky from the north-east and the stars were obscured. We walked down the road in the direction of our hotel. As we got halfway something caught in the back of my throat and I coughed. And then we were in it. A dense cloud of smoke surrounded us. It doubled the silence. You could not hear the insects or other sounds of the night. It stung the eyes, nose and throat. For some reason we didn't stop, but carried on walking. The taste was one of a metallic chemical, almost like the burning of rubber but not as intense. There must have been a fire, perhaps in the old town, but that was fifteen kilometres away. The only building that was close enough that could create such smoke was the hotel. We walked on, T-shirts up round our faces, breathing heavily. The lights from the hotel stood out like the beams of a lighthouse in the fog. The smoke increased.

At the door was a leather-jacketed man with a walkie-talkie. On seeing us he stood aside and opened the door. I asked him where all the smoke was coming from. He shrugged and pointed to the sky and in broken English said, 'Mosquito'. The worst disease you can catch from a mosquito in Cuba is Dengue fever, or to use its more common name, 'break bone fever'. This a more apt description of what it is meant to feel like. It was rare to catch it from a bite here, but someone obviously didn't think so. The smell of the smoke hung in the vents of the hotel and as we went up the lift I wasn't convinced at all by the gateman's explanation. From our window you could barely make out the changing-rooms around the swimming pool only fifty yards away. The lights of Havana in the distance were invisible. I switched off the air-conditioning unit to stop us from being gassed and went to wash my eyes. As we fell asleep I could hear the scuttling of the cockroaches in the unit. They were the only creatures who seemed to be unaffected by the cloud that surrounded the 'Old Man'.

I had only been asleep for a second, or so it seemed, when I was awoken a couple of hours later. There were voices shouting in the corridor and the sound of running feet. I leapt out of bed and pulled the door open. There were four men, all with walkie-talkies, two standing by the lift shaft and the other two at either end of the corridor. When I opened the door they froze. We all just stood and looked at each other. And then they shrank away, back down the stairs and out of sight. No explanation. In all the excitement the smell in the air hadn't registered, but it came over me again as I shut the door. Someone, somewhere was burning something bad. But the fire alarm, if there was one, was not ringing. D was flat out. I yawned and pulled the sheets back over me. I was suddenly very tired.

I slept and I dreamt. The taste of the smoke in my mouth filled every corner of the dream . . . A man is on Hungerford Bridge, one late winter morning in the late '80s. He is walking towards his office. His stride is still as proud as it always has been, head up, shoulders back, free arm swinging in time. The crowd is slow and out of step. This always annoys him. What should be a march of no more than ten minutes takes twenty at this pace. With the drop in pace his mind begins to wander. In fact, this morning it needs no encouragement or invitation. The front of every newspaper on the train up to London did that for him. The headlines screamed in the tabloids and raised their voices on the broadsheets. Two English soldiers had been pulled from their car on the edge of an IRA funeral, stripped, beaten and killed. He did not need the headlines to tell him, however, as a graphic photograph of the bodies in grainy black and white dominated the page. The rage that the man felt was unequalled by any he had felt before. It was not something he had any control over, nor did he wish to have. He rarely lost his temper. But as he waited for the crowd to descend the steps at the other side of the bridge, he could not get the picture out of his head. He felt sick with anger. It was as if he could smell the bodies. Here he was, stuck on a bridge, the rifle that should have been in his hand replaced by a briefcase. Christ, he could murder a smoke.

I awoke, my eyes stinging, and stepped out of bed. A couple of cockroaches had fallen through the grille of the air-conditioning unit and lay stranded on their backs on the polished concrete floor. They had obviously been there for a while as their legs were moving slowly now, as they writhed to right themselves. I picked them up in a tissue and their bodies crackled as I crushed them. I flushed their brown shells and yellow blood down the toilet. I walked over to the window and pulled back the curtain. The fog had vanished leaving no physical trace of its presence, just an insidious nag in the memory. A pale sun was rising over the silhouette of the town in the distance. The sea, to my left, was alive with white horses and was steely blue, almost black in colour. For the first time since I'd arrived in Cuba I felt cold. There was no chance we'd get out in that, but it was worth a go. As I turned around I knocked a glass off the table behind me. It smashed on the floor. On checking out, I mentioned the breakage to the man at reception. He smiled and shrugged and said, 'No worry. As if you no exist. Can go.'

For All Those Left Behind

When we got down to the dock master's office by the quayside, I was even less optimistic about our chances of fishing and was already making plans in my head as to what to do with the day ahead. Inside the office, there were a couple of yacht owners in their fifties or sixties, dressed in satin baseball jackets, ill-fitting jeans that hung off their arses, and baseball caps. They had expensive watches on their wrists, great lumps of gold and, in broad American accents, were discussing the bad attitude of the prostitutes they'd shared the night before. No wonder they called it the Bay of Pigs. The helpful Mayling, a Chino-Cuban woman who I'd spoken to earlier in the week, was on her day off. A man emerged from the dock master's door and, ignoring the men, asked what we wanted. Of course we could go fishing, he told us, there was a low-pressure system due to cross the north of the island at lunchtime, but in the meantime there was no reason why the boat could not go out. There'd be a price, though, $285 for four hours. I wondered how much the two men had paid for their schoolgirls. Probably a fraction of that.

Our skipper was Guillermo and our mate was Ernetto. They smiled as we boarded their boat and every movement spoke of confidence. Ernetto kept nodding and saying, 'Wahoo, the wahoo, we hunt the wahoo.' The wahoo is a vicious, predatory tiger of a fish. Named after one of the small atolls that make up the Sandwich Islands, the largest of which is Hawaii, it grows to a maximum weight of 200 pounds, that of a full-grown man. The body is a lithe barrel of muscle, with silver scales and a blue back striped with bold white bars that look like the work of a branding iron. There is a long spined dorsal fin, a pair of anal fins, and sets of bony fins that run down to the tail, which is more bone than flesh and reminiscent of a shark's. It is this, combined with the shape of the fish, that enables it to run even faster than a marlin, reaching speeds of up to 80 kilometres an hour. Its gills are like iron traps. The mouth is brutally economic: the stark smile of V-shaped jaws, intense red flesh lined with sets of sandpaper-like teeth, that would seem to burn before they bite. The eyes are those of a madman, stolen perhaps from a drowning eighteenth-century sailor, diseased and out of his head. They do not belong on a fish. This crested prince swims in shoals, between the Tropics, where the lips of the reef and inner waters shelve off into the deeps. In the absence of the king of them all, the marlin, the wahoo was a fitting consolation.

Before the boat could leave the marina, we had to hand our passports in for checking at the coastguard's house. Our boat was a powerful cruiser, capable of reaching Miami with ease, a large cabin, open space at the stern and a spotting tower above the wheelhouse. Every day Guillermo and Ernetto took guests of the island out to fish in the waters off Havana. They had no passports of their own and if they harboured a desire to break across the Gulf Stream to exile they hid it well. Ernetto in particular looked as if he had been born on the boat. He was probably only about twenty, but he was stockily built, with tattoos of marlin on both arms. Watching him – as he clipped up the outriggers and ran the baited steel hand lines out behind us, his eyes fixed to the horizon, cigarette clasped between his lips, bare feet gripping the floor of the boat as it smashed over the waves – it was easy to tell what he wanted out of life. He wore a T-shirt that commemorated the forty-ninth Hemingway Tournament. On anyone else this would have looked like a false badge of credibility; on him it was like a garland of triumph. He was what he wanted to be, a fisherman. As the boat gunned into the channel and the metal sign for the marina shrank in the distance, I realised that I was standing amid the pages of the book, with a real-life character from the mind of Hemingway by my side.

The weather chart in the dock master's office was updated every day at about five in the afternoon, and tracked the systems due over the next twenty-four hours. That morning the ink drawing of Cuba was crowned by the thorns of a cold front as it crept in from the north-east. In a scrawled hand someone had written:

'Wind: 20–25 mph

Waves: 8–10 ft

Higher in the Gulf Stream.'

It seemed innocuous within the confines of the office, but out in the channel you could feel the force of the front as it approached. Even at six feet the waves were over the side of the boat and in order to troll Guillermo was running at a fair speed. The diesel fumes from the engine spewed from the back, and there was nowhere you could escape them except on top of the cabin in the spotter's tower. It was too rough to sit up there though – if the boat dropped twelve feet between waves, the force of the impact would throw you off. The diesel took over from the cloud of the evening before, licking at the lining of my throat and sucking at my eyes like leeches. We were fishing with four baits – two large plugs trolling on the surface about sixty yards behind us and two artificial squid worked on steel wire at depths of a 150 feet. Each time a cloud rolled across the sun and darkened the sea around us, my heart raced and I was certain we would get a take. But the boat powered on and soon the fumes made me soporific and despondent as the reels stayed silent. Guillermo was taking the boat in a zigzag along the coastline, west of the Marina. The skyline onshore was littered with red-and-white striped chimneys, spilling noxious white clouds into the air. Ernetto knocked another 'Popular' from its blue-and-white striped packet and ducked his head into his hands to light up. My world of fiction was slowly being suffocated in front of me. Before my eyes, the dials above the wheel turned into monitors and on them I thought I could see the green line of a pulse from years before, fighting its way across the screen, its progress slow and laboured, in time with the choking engine.

The following morning I did something I had not done for a long time. It was a Sunday, and it was not only the gentle rivers of England that were tugging at my sleeve but the vestiges of a religion that I'd done my best to escape from all my life. Perhaps I thought that the church would be the refuge for the old colonials who'd stayed on in '58, drinking gin at midday in the knowledge that they had nowhere else to go in the world. But there were no Panama hats amid the pews, just a jumbled collection of tourists and local families. Until a few years previously, the state had banned all religious ceremony and with this in mind, I had a vision of a congregation that would spill into the street. But not even the presence of the bishop with his hour-long sermon could pull them in. There were no candles to spare at the side of the church and after communion I went back to my pew and stayed on my knees for longer than I had done in the whole of my childhood combined. The prayer was long and searching. My shoes were dusty and I was wearing an airtex shirt and a pair of cut-off combat trousers. The words rose up through the roof of the church, *Yoke, Victor, Zebra, Nothing Heard.*

Immediately afterwards we left for the Marina. The sea was calmer than the previous day and this time as well as Ernetto there was a line man, a sure sign that my prayers might be answered. They chattered away, animatedly, as we left the Marina and headed east down the coast. According to popular lore, the most productive times to fish for wahoo are the hours immediately after dawn and immediately before dusk. It is always possible at these times to pick up a giant lone hunter. But in the middle of the afternoon there is also the possibility of coming across a shoal engaged in a competitive feeding frenzy. On occasions like these the fish seize the bait, the rigs and the trace wire in a multiple strike. We sat up on the hatches with Cristals in hand waiting for such a take. Over the radio you could hear the conversations of the coastguard and yachts waiting to come into the Marina. We sped on, the engines rumbling, the north-westerly breeze taking the fumes away from us for once. Either side of the boat flying fish shot across the tops of the waves. Ernetto climbed into the spotting tower. The boat trolled in smooth arcs across the sea, the baits on the surface skipping out every now and again. The other mate worked the lines and changed lures frequently. In the dropping sun, time rolled on. By five, we hadn't had a touch. The storm of the previous day had brought up a lot of weed and the lures were getting clogged up in it. It would be dark within an hour or so. As dusk approached the sea calmed down and turned golden.

Guillermo broke the silence first, shouting to the mates and pointing out to the left of the boat. Two, maybe three hundred yards away, a school of small tuna were being chased through the water. With incredible synchronicity, they leapt all at once, a thousand fish or more, the sun catching their backs. The boat headed towards them and Ernetto worked fast to take the leads off the steel traces so we could fish more lures on the surface. A new expectancy took over on the boat. We were fast on the heels of the dusk. If we were to catch a wahoo it would be now. I stood between the hatches and watched the water intently. Directly in front of me was a chair made of cream leather with padded arms and wooden slats for its back. It was sunk into the deck by a steel pole. In this chair was where battles against great fish were won and lost. Engaged in a long fight, the angler could not expect to leave it for hours. Buckets of sea water would be poured over them to cool them during the struggle. Such a contest was like a medical operation. The falling sun now lit the sea like a white fire. Against it all I could see was a silhouette of the chair. A sombre quiet fell over the boat as Guillermo turned her and headed back into the Marina. The chair was empty, as useless as a redundant operating table.

It was our last day in Cuba and our flight to London was not due to leave until midnight. I couldn't face getting back into the boat. It was futile. Instead we took a cab out through the back of the docks, past the railway station that looked like a set from *Heaven's Gate*, and south towards the suburb of San Franciso de Paula. Here, up on a crest of a hill, along a driveway overgrown with Bougainvillaea was La Vigia, home to Ernest Hemingway for twenty years between 1940 and 1960. All visitors are denied entrance to the house as it is preserved as a national monument and museum, but it is possible to walk around and peer in through the windows. There, on the walls, were huge faded posters advertising bullfights in northern

Spain, and in one corner a wooden magazine rack full of titles like *The Field* and *The Angler*. On a table, between two easy chairs, were dusty bottles of Campari, uncleaned in forty years. In a bedroom, shelf upon shelf of books, and standing on one, a typewriter, its keys still and seized up with time. At each window a face would stare back at you – a buffalo in one room, an antelope in another. Everywhere, there were books. I shut my eyes and listened for voices, but could only hear the wind blowing through the shutters, the click-clack of dogs' claws on the wooden floor – and the sound of typewriter keys stabbing out their letters onto a fresh page. They spelt out a definite message, one that I had begun to suspect for a while. In the late '30s a man had stepped off a boat in Havana and bought a house for his family. He had two sons. He drove into town on certain days and took up residence in La Floridita. He fished out of Cojimar and fell into the arms of his newly adopted country. Exile was good to him. But another man had continued the voyage on, with his two sons, towards England, his new home, for whom he was a soldier preparing for war. People were keen for him to let his sons go back to Ireland with their mother to avoid the coming conflict. But his sons were adamant, they wanted to stay. In fact, at the age of twelve there was nothing more that Kevin Edward Patrick wanted than to be a soldier of the King rather than a child of Ireland.

I realised that in bereavement you build utopias to replace the memories that fade. Perfect places, aided by fiction in which yourself and the ghosts, real and imagined, live together side by side, marooned in confusion. I looked again into the room and heard nothing.

Chapter Thirteen

Seek? More than that: create. It (the mind) is face to face with something which does not yet exist, to which it alone can give reality and substance, which it alone can bring into the light of day.

Remembrance of Things Past, Marcel Proust

Had I done this? Was my search something which I was latently guiding, a quest whose fulfilment I had in some way already planned? If it was, or if indeed, it ever had been, I would have surely ended it in Cuba. When I sat on the plane during the outward journey to Havana I had a distinct vision in my head, one which I had been nurturing for months. I was on a boat, somewhere far out in the Gulf Stream, the temperature high up in the thirties. The sun was like a wall of light. The water rolled gently in a holy dance. The rods were set with the lines paying out into the deep but the boat's engine was still. About 100 yards behind us, a figure was walking towards the boat. It was my father, dressed in a light-blue towelling open-necked T-shirt, a pair of fawn linen chinos and his desert boots. The sun shone off the face of his Diving

Star watch as he gradually drew closer. Instead of fading as he got nearer, the image grew stronger and before I knew it he was aboard and we were standing side by side. The engine started up and the boat was away. There is much laughter between us, we even share a cigarette together, our conversation flowing quickly and leaping off at over-enthusiastic tangents. Life is so full and colourful and yet in description it comes down to a few events and a few dates. It is hard for me to describe all the habits I have inherited and how, each time when one appears, it is him and him alone whom I think of. Sometimes I feel as if they are taking over my days and turning me into him. I question him over and over again and occasionally he avoids the issue by reaching into the cabin, handing me another beer and then saying nothing. There are fish all around us, leaping through the waves and swimming around the boat. I have no desire to fish for them at all. I realise that they are his guardians as much as he is mine.

And now, on the plane back to London, I know that this vision was just a wish. A cancer had killed my father. Malignant cells attacking healthy ones until the internal organs ceased to function. A guerrilla war within one's own body. A killer you can keep in a jar. Once I had been sick of telling people of how my father had died. Now I had reached the point where they no longer asked, and I realised that, previously, it was probably me who'd brought it up in the first place. Ever since I had locked it away with the passing years, but it was still there. It bred a fear that was out of character; a thin, trapping gauze that wound its way around every hope and shard of optimism. The fear was almost a replica of a tumour itself. It would not debilitate me in the same way but it would alter the choices I made and that in turn would affect the quality of my life. Yes, a cancer killed my father, but I was certain that something had triggered it, set the timer ticking slowly some years before. I longed for some form of exorcism to prevent the hereditary trap being set again; to guard against the inherited anger and sorrow that were somewhere deep in me, mutating into the cells of a fresh disease.

It is 1966 in the village of Liss in Hampshire. There is a house with a red gabled roof and a lean-to conservatory, whose glass is held together by thin struts of white painted wood. In front of the house is a lawn and up the side of this a red cinder-and-ash path boxed in by planks of wood on either side. This path runs along the side of the house to a door. The door leads into a passageway, which in my memory is dark and shadowy. Leading off from this to one side is a small room with a bay window that looks out over the narrow path. By the window is a wooden table and behind it an old chest of drawers that has been painted green. Each drawer contains the linen for the house. This is washed religiously every Monday by Lily Andrews, despite the arthritic rheumatism that makes her hands swell and crack. On Mondays the smell of steaming water and melting soap flakes exhumes the stale lingering veil of cigarette smoke that fills the house for the rest of the week. At the end of the room is a tiny kitchen with a gas cooker and butler sink. To one side is a walk-in pantry. On the floor is a collection of beer bottles, unopened, their stone stoppers shut tight on the neck. At the back is a rack of vegetables, potatoes mostly, and on one of the shelves a jug of milk. With these, Lily cooks her favourite meal, the one she swears she could live on – boiled potatoes and a glass of milk.

Inside this room two people sit and chatter away. They are Lily Andrews and her husband, Teddy. On the table is a china mug full of tea and a Pyrex glass half-full of pale ale. They talk and light up, the conversation darting in and out, contradiction, interruption, laughter. Their talk is of family, of the grandchild who will be born in the winter and of the relations they haven't seen for decades. There is delight and shock in equal measure. They sit for hours and the kettle is refilled and another stone stopper broken. Outside the room, the hallway is dark. Off it, to one side, are two rooms, the larger of which is filled with the best furniture that was brought home from Burma. There are photographs and paintings framed on the wall and a clock that stands on the mantelpiece above the fire. The fire is unlit, but the grate is swept and ready, filled with paper, kindling and coalite. In the silence of the room the gentle ticking of the clock marks time. This is the best room, the one they use only on special occasions. It is not lived in on a daily basis. Next to it is a smaller living-room, a snug of sorts. In it are a couple of armchairs, a table with a collection of newspapers lying on it and in the corner a Ferguson television. On Saturday afternoons Teddy sits in here and watches the horse racing on the grainy black-and-white picture, urging the riders on. For now its screen is grey and silent, the silver dials asleep.

Beyond the two rooms is a door, framed by a wooden porchway which leads out into a small garden. Next to the door is a staircase. At the top of the stairs is a bathroom and three bedrooms. In each of them the window is open at the top and the cool air of the evening settles on the eiderdowns that lie on the beds. The light is fading and the rooms seem gloomy. It is as if the house is empty. But downstairs in the room by the kitchen, Lily and Teddy are still talking away, their conversation a rattle of words and exclamation. In the bay window, you can see their reflections against the glass. The yellow glow from the light that hangs down from the ceiling shines through the fug and illuminates them. This is their new home, one small room far away from the country where they were born. It is a place of gladness, safety and comfort. Back outside this room, in the growing darkness that is encompassing the rest of the house, is the echo of a distant shout that is barely audible. It is a mixture of reproach and regret, the spores and dust of secrets carried on a summer wind across the sea from Ireland. In the twilight you can almost see it.

This house called Red Gables stood on St Mary's Road with the church of the same name at the head of it. St Mary's was Church of England. On 30 January 1992 we buried my own father away from St Mary's on the edge of the village of Liss in the west cemetery, built allegedly for the Catholics. He lay thirty metres from the grave of his mother and father. Lily Andrews died of lung cancer in May of 1969 and Teddy Andrews of emphysema in the January of 1973. Every day after Lily's death, Teddy would catch the train to Petersfield to hear mass and on his return he would cross the road by the station and have a drink in the Crossing Gate public house. The Crossing Gate had two bars – the station bar on the left with its lino flooring and outside toilets across the car park, and the saloon bar, carpeted, with its tables and chairs under the windows. At midday on any day between 1969 and 1973 you would find Thomas Edward Andrews at the bar of one of these, a pint of Courage in one hand and a burning cigarette in the other. Routine was becoming harder now it was just him; by lunchtime it seemed everything had been done and the afternoon simply stretched out ahead. A pint seemed to speed up the hands of the clock and slow down the pursuit of memory. There was nothing left for the horsemen of exile to hunt down now that Lily was gone, and he could not care if they came at last for him. His sons were British soldiers, but more important than that they were sons of this gentle unassuming English county of Hampshire. He knew it when he looked into their eyes and when he heard them speak. He and Lily hadn't done a bad job after all, turning exile into escape in the space of one generation. Once in a while, when he stayed for another drink and the afternoon light spilled in through the window he would look around the bar. He would close his eyes and hear the lilt of voices, the shouts and laughter of men on market day. Before him he could see the circle of musicians as they jostled for space and kicked the boxes for their instruments under their chairs with their large leather shoes. The music would start up and Teddy would open his eyes. He could only see fully out of the left one, the right having been damaged many years before by a breech explosion in a shotgun. It was funny how in your memory you always saw with both, he thought. The station bar was always empty at this time, and he knew that soon that he should go, too.

It was February 2001. I parked the car in St Mary's Road and walked with Deborah down towards the railway line. Our Lady calls every Catholic back and I should have known that the end of my fishing odyssey would lie somewhere near here. Over a small bridge under which a small river ran in spate, its water brown and frothy, and I was outside the Crossing Gate. The door to the station bar was closed but the one to the saloon was open. I walked in and up to the bar. Aside from the barman and his wife there was no one else in the pub. The barman looked up and I hesitated, 'A pint of Courage and a glass of lemonade, please.'

'The Courage is off. The barrel's being changed.'

'I'll have the other, then,' I said, pointing to the tap. The gush of a fresh pint being pulled filled the glass. The barman set the pint on the bar top and poured the lemonade from a bottle behind him. For a brief moment the liquid appeared to turn red. I blinked and looked at it again. It was clear, without even a trace of pink, let alone red. I felt surprised and could not stop staring at it.

The roach is a gregarious fish; that is to say, it swims in shoals. As a species, it is to be found in almost any waters in England, as frequently in the tiniest of wayland ponds as in one of the Norfolk Broads or in The Thames. Its area of distribution is: Britain, as far north as Loch Lomond and the Teith (it is scarce in Devon, Cornwall, and West Wales); Europe, north of the Pyrenees and Alps; Russian Turkestan and Siberia. It does not occur in Ireland.

Edward Ensom ('Faddist')

The scales of a roach can change colour depending on the environment in which the fish lives. They are essentially silver, but can have a blue or even a brown hue to them. The fins, though, are always red, particularly those that grow from under the belly. It was of the roach that I had thought more and more since returning from Cuba. The fish had taken on an almost religious, iconic character. Whenever I pictured it, I saw it removed from its environment and backlit by a silver star, lying on a background of purple or red velvet. It was to all effects becoming a saint. I wanted to fish for this now, and this alone.

The winter is the best time, in angling lore at least, to fish for the roach. It is starved of its natural foods, caddis larvae and wasp grubs, bloodworms and silkweed. The cold water cleans the flanks and rids it of leeches and suckers and there is every chance of catching that rarity, a specimen of over two pounds. A small fish in relation to the tench, chub or the carp, but no less pure and precious.

But this winter was savage. The rain had started falling in October and had not stopped for months. It had been four feet over its average at Temple House Lake in November; I now expected it to be lapping at the door of the house. The rivers of England had burst their banks on dozens of occasions and flooded the fields around them. At its close, the autumn of the year 2000 was claimed as the wettest since records began in 1783. Every new enquiry I made about fishing was rebuffed with a laugh of derision or replied to with stern warnings about how the overhanging banks were waiting to be swept away. I longed for a high-pressure system so I could take Dad for that final walk along a river bank on a crisp, blue winter's morning. I knew now that the river should be in Hampshire, his adopted county.

The season would end at midnight on 14 March and as February slipped by I grew anxious that I would not be able to keep our appointment. The River Rother flows right through the village of Liss but even after nights of phone calls I was unable to find out who controlled the stretch and from whom I would need permission to fish it. I did find out that it was owned by a syndicate, but no one knew how to get in touch with them. Even so, it would have still been closed to me, as one more flood took its waters up over the bridge and onto the roads. But there was still one place where it was possible to fish for the roach and even to come home with a specimen of two pounds. I sat alone in a pub round the corner from Phillips Auction House in west London. It was 11.30 a.m. and the sky outside was a vivid blue. A high pressure had blown down from the north and at last I had my winter's morning. On the television screen in the corner a horse race began with the clank and thud of gates being lifted automatically above the riders' heads. I had £700 in cash tucked into the inside pocket of my Moss Bros British Army warm and a half-empty pint of bitter in front of me. In my hand was a catalogue for a sale of Fishing Tackle and Piscatoriana. There were several fine roach in the sale, each one illustrated by a black-and-white photographic portrait. One case in particular had caught my eye. It was lot number 283 and the catalogue described it as:

> An extremely rare golden roach by J. Cooper & Sons, mounted in a setting of reeds and grasses against a light blue background in a gilt lined bow

front case with card to interior inscribed 'Golden Roach. Taken from the River Frays. Oct 8th 1911'.

*Specimens of golden coloured roach caught in the wild are extremely rare, a letter reporting such a catch from the Ribble appeared in the 19 September 1931 *Fishing Gazette*. In response the British museum described the unusual colouration as due to a condition known as xanthochroism rarely found in the wild in which only the red and yellow pigment is developed, the black and brown almost entirely lacking.

Guide price £1000–£1500.

A golden roach. A rare one, without a trace of black and tan. My golden calf. With him on my wall I had no need of a crucifix and could say my stations of the cross with each cast.

I crept into the sale an hour later and the room was full of dealers and collectors. The bidding was fast, with the auctioneer getting through about 120 lots in an hour. I took a seat as far to the back of the room as possible and waited. The roach was the first of the cased lots and as its sale approached the palms of my hands began to sweat. With about fifteen lots still to go, a man stood up behind me and went over to the wall where the fish were hanging. Next to the roach was a pike of thirty pounds taken from the Royalty Fishery on the Hampshire Avon. The man took great interest in this and the roach. I scrutinised his every move whilst hoping that he would not catch my eye. And then, suddenly, we were only one lot away. The sweat was now running down my back. My bidding card was number

419. The auctioneer read out the description of the fish from the catalogue and a colleague pointed it out to the floor. They started at £600. Nobody moved. I gripped the card tightly between my fingers but I did not want to raise it just yet. The auctioneer called again at £600. Still nothing. I began to move my arm when I heard the words, 'At the very back of the room I have six hundred,' and that was enough. The auctioneer drove the bids up, past seven, past eight and nine hundred and onto one thousand. My arm was suspended in mid-air, in a half-hearted non-bid. The fish had gone to the man at the back of the room. He spent another £3,000 on further lots and then left quietly. I felt sick, but I knew I hadn't given myself a real chance. After all, its guide started at one thousand.

There was one roach left. It was not golden, did not appear to possess any holy properties and it did not even have a name or date. It was lot number 357, described as:

> A roach in the style of Cooper, mounted in a setting
> of reeds and grasses against a light blue background
> in a gilt lined bow front case. c. 1900.
> Guide price £150–£250.

No one bid against me this time. As the bid closed, I looked to the front of the auction room but it had changed suddenly into the interior of a church. The auctioneer had become a priest. I watched as he took a similar card to mine with the same number, 419, and slid it into the wooden hymn board at the front of the church. I looked down at my catalogue and it had turned into a hymn book,

For All Those Left Behind

No goblin nor foul fiend
can daunt his spirit;
he knows he at the end
shall life inherit.

Words from a version of Bunyan's 'To be a Pilgrim'. The hymn we sang at the mass of my father's funeral had found its number.

———— · ————

After the sale I paid up at the cashier's window and went to collect the fish. The case's black, japanned wood was splintered and chipped. On one side the glass panel had been cracked. It was held together by a strip of Sellotape, which was brittle and brown. Looking at it, I guessed the roach was just over the two-pound mark. I loved it even more for its anonymity, for it could have come from any number of Hampshire shoals and you would not have known the difference. As there was no name inscribed in gilt on the front of the case it was as if I had caught it myself.

If I had paid a bit more attention during the sermons of my childhood I would have known that real saints travelled in the clothes of the day and that it was the false emperors who were decorated in gold robes. They, too, lived in palaces where the windows stayed unbroken for 100 years. An impossible vision of a life, every scale in place, each fin in sail, polished and perfect. Yes, this kind of immortality was only possible in a vacuum, sealed off beyond decay.

I had sought and in a way I had created. I had a prince of Ireland, a pike, and a son of England, a roach, boxed, mounted and immortalised over fireplaces in my home. The two were under my roof at last, the one unable to chase and kill the other. Like ashes on the mantel. An exorcism, a truce. Between them they had a sense of power, one that could dissolve the cancerous organs that were bottled up somewhere on a dusty shelf. As they disintegrated so did the sadness my father, and his before him, had carried with them – that wrench of leaving home, the army for one, a country for the other. The beautiful pike I'd taken from Temple House was a blessing from my grandfather, a token from his childhood in Sligo. I had thought at the time that it was the murmur of my father's lung that I had felt in the boat, but I knew now it was my grandfather's as he struggled with emphysema. On one of his many walks back to Red Gables from the Crossing Gate perhaps he thought of his grandson fishing, one day, back in Sligo. That pike was Ireland to me and to all of our family, beauty and danger, no wonder when its young ate each other people called it the Union Jack.

Most importantly of all I had learnt to seek the roach. The symbol of one last promise from my father. Buried at the back of loss, telling me that identity wasn't found in one place or in one form, but in a question that should always be asked by successive generations. I'd first asked it on that humid summer's evening as my father drove us out towards Lodge Pond.

'What will we be fishing for tonight, Dad?'

He turned to me, smiled, and placed his hand upon my head.

'What most people fish for, son. Roach and lots of other things too, you'll see.'

207

Credits

Page 32 Extract from *The Gentleman's Recreation* by Nicholas Cox (1674)

Page 88 Extract from 'The Cuillin' by Sorley MacLean appeared originally in *From Wood to Ridge*. Reproduced courtesy of Carcanet Press Limited

Page 91 Extract from *In Search of Scotland* by H.V. Morton. Reproduced courtesy of Methuen Publishing Limited. Copyright © Marion Wadsell & Brian de Villiers

Page 111 Extract from Phillips Auctioneers Catalogue. Reproduced courtesy of Bonhams, formerly Phillips

Page 112 Extracts from the *Sunday Telegraph* 16 November 1986

Page 131 Extract from 'The Meditation of the Old Fisherman' by W.B. Yeats, taken from *W.B. Yeats – Poems selected by Seamus Heaney*. Faber and Faber 2000. Reproduced courtesy of A.P. Watt Ltd on behalf of Michael B. Yeats

Page 137 Extract from *Ireland: A History* by Robert Kee. Reproduced courtesy of Weidenfeld and Nicolson (Illustrated)

Page 151 Extract from *Islands in the Stream* by Ernest Hemingway. Reproduced courtesy of HarperCollins Publishers Ltd Copyright (©) (1970) (Ernest Hemingway)

Page 165 Extract from *The Pocket Oxford Dictionary of Current English* compiled by F.G. Fowler and H.W. Fowler (1924). Reproduced courtesy of Oxford University Press.

Page 180 Extract from *The Pocket Oxford Dictionary of Current English* compiled by F.G. Fowler and H.W. Fowler (1924). Reproduced courtesy of Oxford University Press.

Page 195 Extract from *Rememberance of Things Past* by Marcel Proust, translated by C.K. Scott-Moncrieff and Terence Kilmartin. Reproduced by permission of The Random House Group Ltd

Page 201 Quotation by Edward Ensom ('Faddist') appeared originally in *Fine Angling for Coarse Fish* – Seeley, Service & Co. Limited 1947. Every effort has been made by the author to trace the owners of Edward Ensom's copyright. The owners are invited to contact the author via Mainstream Publishing Co (Edinburgh) Ltd, 7 Albany Street, Edinburgh, EH1 3UG

Page 203 Extract from Phillips Auctioneers Catalogue. Reproduced courtesy of Bonhams, formerly Phillips

Page 205 Extract from Phillips Auctioneers Catalogue. Reproduced courtesy of Bonhams, formerly Phillips

Page 206 Extract from 'To be a Pilgrim' After John Bunyan (1628–88) *Hymns Ancient and Modern Revised* (1950) (Hymns Ancient and Modern Ltd)